Foundation

MATHEMATICS

GCSE for AQA

Homework Book

Nick Asker and Karen Morrison

CAMBRIDGE
UNIVERSITY PRESS

University Printing House, Cambridge CB2 8BS, United Kingdom

Cambridge University Press is part of the University of Cambridge.

It furthers the University's mission by disseminating knowledge in the pursuit of
education, learning and research at the highest international levels of excellence.

www.cambridge.org

Information on this title:
www.cambridge.org/ukschools/9781107496910 (Paperback)

First published 2015
Reprinted 2016

Printed in Poland by Opolgraf

A catalogue record for this publication is available from the British Library

ISBN 978-1-107-49691-0 Paperback

Additional resources for this publication at www.cambridge.org/ukschools

Cover image © 2013 Fabian Oefner www.fabianoefner.com

....

Contents

Introduction

This book has been written by experienced teachers to help you practise applying the skills and knowledge you will learn during your GCSE course.

Each chapter is divided into sections, which cover individual topics. A section contains one or more homework exercises, containing a range of questions so you can apply your knowledge of the topic. At the end of each chapter, the Chapter review contains a mixture of questions covering all of the topics in the chapter.

Look out for the following features throughout the book:

 This means you might need a calculator to work through a question.

 This means you should work through a question without using a calculator. If this is not present, you can use a calculator if you need to.

Tip

Tip boxes provide helpful hints.

The Homework Book chapters and sections match those of the *GCSE Mathematics for AQA Foundation Student Book*, so you can easily use the two books alongside each other. However, you can also use the Homework Book without the Student Book.

You can check your answers using the free answer booklet available at **www.cambridge.org/ukschools/ gcsemaths-homeworkanswers**.

1 Working with integers

Section 1: Basic calculations

HOMEWORK 1A

**Solve these problems using written methods.
Set out your solutions clearly to show the methods
you chose.**

1. How many 12 litre containers can be completely
filled from a tanker containing 783 litres?

2. A train is travelling at a constant speed of
64 mph.
   a How far does it travel in $1\frac{1}{2}$ hours?
   b How long does it take to travel 336 miles?

Tip
64 mph means the train travels 64 miles
each hour.

3. A train starts a journey with 576 people on
board. At the first station 23 people get on,
14 get off. At the second station 76 people get
off and no one gets on. At the third station a
further 45 people get on.
How many people are on the train after the
third station?

4. What is the product of 19 and 21?

5. Which of the following pairs of numbers has a
difference of 37 and a product of 2310?
   a 23 and 60   b 77 and 30
   c 66 and 35   d 33 and 70

Tip
Use trial, error and improvement.

HOMEWORK 1B

1. The temperature one day in Aberdeen is 3 °C.
Overnight the temperature drops by 11 °C.
What is the temperature the next morning?

2. Calculate:
   a $13 - 4 + 8$ b $-4 - 3 - 7$ c $-5 + 9 - 6$
   d $-8 - (-5) + 3$ e $-27 + (-12) - 18$

3. Simplify:
   a $-2 \times -5 \times -3$ b $-3 \times 8 \times -2$
   c $8 \times -4 \times 7$ d $-8 \times -6 \times -4 \times 3$
   e $-48 \div 12$ f $-144 \div -8$
   g $424 \div -8$ h $-225 \div -15$

Tip
Make sure you know the rules about
multiplying and dividing by negative numbers.

4. Simplify:
   a $\dfrac{40}{8}$ b $\dfrac{63}{-9}$ c $\dfrac{-81}{-9}$ d $\dfrac{-200}{8}$ e $\dfrac{-360}{-9}$

5. Hilary's business account has £489 in the bank
on a Sunday night.
Calculate the missing figures to complete the
table below.

Day	Spends	Deposits	Balance
Monday	£456	£745	
Tuesday		£398	−£100
Wednesday	£1109		£33

6. Here is a set of integers: $-7, -5, -1, 2, 7, 11$
   a Find two numbers with a difference of 7
   b Find two numbers with a product of -7
   c Find three numbers with a sum of 4

Section 2: Order of operations

HOMEWORK 1C

1. Calculate the following.
   a $6 \times 11 + 4$ b $6 \times (11 - 2)$
   c $5 + 11 \times 2$ d $(3 + 12) \times 4$
   e $25 + 6 \times 3$ f $8 \times 3 \div (4 + 2)$
   g $(14 + 7) \div 3$ h $43 + 2 \times 8 + 6$
   i $24 \div 4 \times (8 - 5)$ j $16 - \dfrac{8}{2} + 5$

2 Use the numbers listed (in bold) to make each number sentence true.

a $\boxed{} - \boxed{} \div \boxed{} = \boxed{}$ 1, 18, 6, 4

b $\boxed{} - \boxed{} \div \boxed{} = \boxed{}$ 8, 7, 3, 2

c $\boxed{} \div (\boxed{} - \boxed{}) - \boxed{} = \boxed{}$ 2, 3, 4, 7, 15

Tip

Learn the rules about order of operations.

Section 3: Inverse operations

HOMEWORK 1D

1 Find the additive inverse of each of these numbers.

a 7   **b** 6   **c** 200   **d** −7   **e** −21   **f** −36

2 By what number would you multiply each of these to get an answer of 1?

a 4   **b** 12   **c** −5   **d** $\dfrac{1}{2}$ **e** 7   **f** $\dfrac{1}{8}$

3 Use inverse operations to check the results of each calculation.
Correct those that are incorrect.

a $6247 - 1907 = 4340$ **b** $2487 - 1581 = 816$
c $7845 - 2458 = 547$ **d** $4588 + 2549 = 7137$

4 Use inverse operations to find the missing values in each of these calculations.

a $\boxed{} + 564 = 729$

b $\boxed{} + 389 = 786$

c $\boxed{} - 293 = 146$

d $132 \times \boxed{} = -3564$

e $-8 \times \boxed{} = 392$

f $\boxed{} \div 30 = 4800$

Chapter 1 review

1 Bonita and Kim travel for three and a half hours at 48 kilometres per hour.
They then travel a further 53 km.
What is the total distance they have travelled?

2 On a page of a newspaper there are eight columns of text.
Each row contains a maximum of 38 characters (spaces between words count as characters).
Each column has a total of 168 rows.

a What is the maximum number of characters that can appear on a page?

b The average word length is six characters, and each word needs a space after it.
Estimate the number of words that can fit on a page.

3 A theatre has seats for 2925 people. How many rows of 75 is this?

4 Two numbers have a sum of −12 and a product of −28. What are the numbers?

5 Jadheja's bank account was overdrawn. She deposited £750 and this brought her balance to £486. By how much was her account overdrawn to start with?

2 Collecting, interpreting and representing data

Section 1: Populations and samples

HOMEWORK 2A

1 A local shop owner wants to find out how many boxes of a new crisp flavour she should order.

She asks the first ten customers who come into the shop whether they would buy the new flavour if she started selling them.

a What is the population in this survey?

b What is the sample involved in the survey?

c Is this a representative sample or not?
Give a reason for your answer.

2 Sami says: 'More and more people are using texts these days instead of phoning and talking to each other.' How could you collect data to find out whether this statement is true or not? Include details about the sources of your data and the sample size.

3 The statements below show you what four students found out when they collected data.

Student A 30% of heart disease is caused by smoking.

Student B 79% of all dustbin contents is recyclable.

Student C Most people spend between £5 and £10 per day on transport.

Student D Almost $\frac{2}{3}$ of the women at my mum's workplace say that men earn more than they do.

a What question do you think each student was trying to answer?

b What sources of information do you think each student used to find their data?

c How do you think student D selected a random sample from her mum's workplace?

Section 2: Tables and charts
HOMEWORK 2B

1 Nika tossed a dice 40 times and got these results.

```
6  6  6  5  4  3  2  6  5  4
1  1  3  2  5  4  3  3  3  2
1  6  5  5  4  4  3  2  5  4
6  3  2  4  2  1  2  2  1  5
```

a Copy and complete this frequency table to organise the data.

Score	1	2	3	4	5	6
Frequency						

b Do the results suggest that this is a fair dice or not? Give a reason for your answer.

2 Study the diagram carefully and answer the questions about it.

Number of students in each year

Key: 👤 = 30 students

a What type of chart is this?
b What does the chart show?
c What does each full symbol represent?
d How are 15 students shown on the chart?
e How many students are there in Year 8?
f Which year group has the most students? How many are there in this year group?
g Do you think these are accurate or rounded figures? Why?

3 The table shows the population (in millions) of five of the world's largest cities.

City	Tokyo	Seoul	Mexico City	New York	Mumbai
Population (millions)	32.5	20.6	20.5	19.75	19.2

Draw a pictogram to show this data.

4 The frequency table shows the number of people who were treated for road accident injuries in the A & E ward of a large hospital in the first six months of the year. Draw a vertical line chart to represent the data. Use a scale of 1 cm per 50 patients on the vertical axis.

Month	Number of patients
January	360
February	275
March	190
April	375
May	200
June	210

5 Draw a bar chart to show this data.

Favourite takeaway food	Burgers	Kebabs	Fried chicken	Chips	Other
No. of people	40	30	84	20	29

HOMEWORK 2C

1 The table below shows the type of food that a group of students on a camping trip chose for breakfast.

	Cereal	Hot porridge	Bread
Girls	8	16	12
Boys	2	12	10

   a Draw a single bar chart to show the choice of cereal against bread.

   b Draw a compound bar chart to show the breakfast food choice for girls and boys.

2 The favourite subjects of a group of students is shown in the table.

Subject	Girls	Boys
Mathematics	34	33
English	45	40
Biology	29	31
ICT	40	48

   a Draw a double bar graph to show this data.

   b How many girls chose Mathematics?

   c How many boys chose ICT?

   d Which is the favourite subject among the girls?

   e Which subject was chosen as favourite by the fewest boys?

3 A tourist organisation in the Caribbean records how many tourists visit their region each month from the UK and from other countries. Draw a compound bar graph to display the data for the first six months of the year.

	UK visitors	Other visitors
Jan.	12 000	40 000
Feb.	10 000	39 000
Mar.	19 000	15 000
Apr.	16 000	12 000
May	21 000	19 000
Jun.	2 000	25 000

Section 3: Pie charts
HOMEWORK 2D

1 This pie chart shows the colours that 80 students selected as their favourite from a five-colour chart.

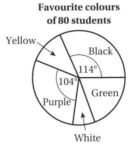

Favourite colours of 80 students

   a Which colour is most popular?

   b Which colour is least popular?

   c What percentage of the students chose purple as their favourite colour?

   d How many students chose black as their favourite colour?

2 This table shows the approximate percentage of the world's population living on each continent.

Africa	Asia	Europe	North America	South America	Oceania
13	61	12	5	8.5	0.5

   a Draw a pie chart to display this data.

   b How else could you display this data?

Section 4: Line graphs for time-series data
HOMEWORK 2E

1 The graphs below represent the average monthly temperature and the average monthly rainfall for Cairo, in Egypt.

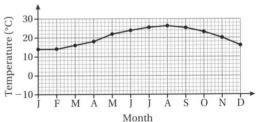

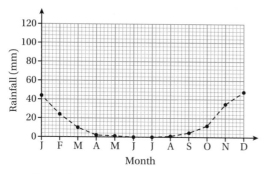

a What is the maximum average temperature?
b In what months is the average temperature above 20 °C?
c Is Egypt in the northern or southern hemisphere?
d Is the temperature ever below freezing point?
e What is the average rainfall in November?
f In which month is the average rainfall 2 mm?
g Looking at both graphs, what can you say about the rainfall when the temperatures are high?

2 Amy bought a new car in 2010. Its value over time is shown below.

Year	Value of car
2010	£13 900
2011	£7 000
2012	£5 700
2013	£4 700
2014	£4 000

a Draw a line graph to represent this information.
b What is the percentage depreciation in the first year she owned the car?
c Use your graph to estimate the value of the car in 2015.

3 The table shows the distance (metres) covered by a car travelling at 90 kilometres per hour.

Time (seconds)	40	80	120	160	200
Distance (metres)	1000	2000	3000	4000	5000

Draw a line graph to show this relationship.

Chapter 2 review

1 Michelle collected data about how many children different families in her community had. Her results are shown below.

0	3	4	3	3	2	2	2	2	1	1	1
3	3	4	3	6	2	2	2	0	0	2	1
5	4	3	2	4	3	3	3	2	1	1	0
3	1	1	1	1	0	0	0	2	4	5	3

a How do you think Michelle collected the data?
b Draw up a frequency table, with tallies, to organise the data.
c Represent the data on a pie chart.
d Draw a bar chart to compare the number of families that have three or fewer children with those that have four or more children.

2 Mrs Sanchez bakes and sells biscuits. One week she sells 420 peanut crunchies, 488 chocolate cups and 320 coconut munchies. Draw a pictogram to represent this data.

3 Use data below collected from ten students for this question.

Student	Gender	Height (m)	Eye colour	Hair colour	Siblings
1	F	1.55	Br	Bl	0
2	F	1.61	Gr	Bl	3
3	M	1.63	Gr	Blo	4
4	M	1.60	Br	Br	2
5	M	1.61	Br	Br	1
6	F	1.62	Br	Br	2
7	M	1.64	Br	Bl	3
8	F	1.69	Gr	Bl	1
9	F	1.61	Bl	Bl	0
10	M	1.65	Br	Bl	3

a Draw a pie chart to show the data about the number of siblings.
b Represent the height of students using an appropriate chart.
c Draw a compound bar chart showing eye and hair colour by gender.

4 The diagram below shows global population in given years.

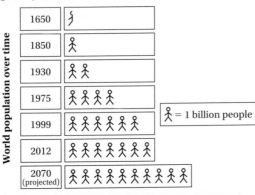

1650	
1850	
1930	
1975	
1999	
2012	
2070 (projected)	

World population over time

⚇ = 1 billion people

a What type of diagram is this?
b What does each symbol represent?
c What was the population of the world in 1650?
d How long did it take the population to double after 1650?
e When did the world's population reach 7 billion?
f The United Nations predicts that the world's population will reach 9.2 billion in 2050. How would you show this on the diagram?
g Redraw this data as a line graph.

3 Analysing data

Section 1: Averages and range
HOMEWORK 3A

1 For each of the frequency distributions (data sets A–C) shown below calculate:
  a the mean score   b the median score
  c the modal score.

Data set A

Score	1	2	3	4	5	6
Frequency	12	14	15	12	15	12

Data set B

Score	10	20	30	40	50	60	70	80
Frequency	13	25	22	31	16	23	27	19

Data set C

Score	1.5	2.5	3.5	4.5	5.5	6.5
Frequency	15	12	15	12	10	21

2 The table shows the number of words per minute typed by a group of computer programmers.

Words per minute (w)	Frequency
$31 \leqslant w < 36$	40
$36 \leqslant w < 41$	70
$41 \leqslant w < 46$	80
$46 \leqslant w < 51$	90
$51 \leqslant w < 56$	60
$56 \leqslant w < 61$	20

a Calculate an estimate for the mean number of words typed per minute.
b How many words do most of the programmers manage to type per minute?
c What is the median class?
d What is the range of words typed per minute?

HOMEWORK 3B

1 Five students scored a mean mark of 14.8 out of 20 for a maths test.
  a Which of these sets of marks fit this mean?
    i 14, 16, 17, 15, 17
    ii 12, 13, 12, 19, 19
    iii 12, 19, 12, 18, 13
    iv 13, 17, 15, 16, 17
    v 19, 19, 12, 0, 19
    vi 15, 15, 15, 15, 14
  b Compare the sets of numbers in your answer above. Give a reason why you can get the same mean from different sets of numbers.

2 Twenty students scored the following results in a test out of 20.

17 18 17 14 8 3 15 18 3 15
0 17 16 17 14 7 18 19 5 15

  a Calculate the mean, median, mode and range of the marks.
  b Why is the median the best summary statistic for this particular set of data?

3 The table below shows the times in minutes and seconds that two runners achieved over 800 m during one season.

Runner A	2 min 2.5 s	2 min 1.7 s	2 min 2.2 s	2 min 3.7 s	2 min 1.7 s	2 min 2.9 s	2 min 2.6 s
Runner B	2 min 2.4 s	2 min 1.8 s	2 min 2.3 s	2 min 4.4 s	2 min 0.6 s	2 min 2.2 s	2 min 1.2 s

a Which runner is the better of the two? Why?
b Which runner is more consistent? Why?

4 Two students get the following results for six mathematical tests which are marked out of 100.

Anna: 60, 90, 100, 90, 90, 100
Zane: 60, 70, 60, 70, 70, 100

a What is the range of scores for each student?
b Does this show they both had equally good results?
c Which statistic would be a better measure of their achievement? Why?

Section 2: Misleading graphs
HOMEWORK 3C

1 This graph shows the number of computers sold by two competing stores over a four month period.

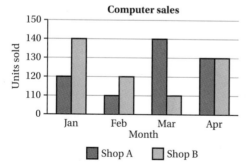

a Did shop B sell double the number of computers that shop A sold in January? Give a reason for your answer.
b Did shop A sell four times as many computers as shop B in March? Give a reason for your answer..
c Calculate the total number of computers sold over the period for each shop. How do the figures compare?
d How is this graph misleading?

2 Study the pie chart below.

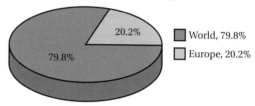

Less than a quarter of the world's internet users are in Europe

a What does the chart suggest to you? Why?
b Europe has 11.5% of the world's population. Does this affect how you interpret this graph? Give a reason for your answer.
c Why should pie charts not be shown with 3D sections?

Section 3: Scatter diagrams
HOMEWORK 3D

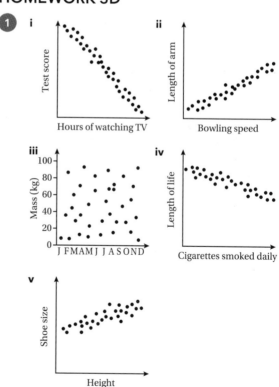

a Describe the correlations shown on the scatter diagrams shown above.
b Copy graphs **i**, **ii**, **iv** and **v** and draw a line of best fit on them.

7

2 Sookie collected data from 15 students in her school athletics team. She wanted to see if there was a correlation between the height of the students and the distance they could jump in the long-jump event. She drew a scatter diagram to show the data as shown below.

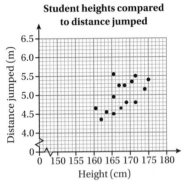

Student heights compared to distance jumped

a Copy the diagram and draw the line of best fit on to it.

b Use your line of best fit to estimate how far a student 165 cm tall could jump.

c For the age group of Sookie's school team, the girls' record for long jump is 6.07 m. How tall would you expect a girl to be who could equal the record jump?

d Describe the correlation shown on the graph.

e What does the correlation indicate about the relationship between height and how far you can jump in the long-jump event?

3 Mrs Andrews wants to know whether her students' results on a mid-year test are a good indication of how well they will do in the GCSE examinations. The results from the test and the examination are given for a group of students.

Student	Mid-year mark	GCSE mark	Student	Mid-year mark	GCSE mark
Anna	78	73	Tina	92	86
Nick	57	51	Yemi	41	50
Sarah	30	39	Asma	75	64
Ahmed	74	80	Rita	84	77
Sanjita	74	74	Mike	55	58
Moeneeb	88	73	Karen	90	80
Kwezi	94	88	James	89	87
Pete	83	69	Priya	95	96
Idowu	70	63	Claudia	67	70
Sam	61	67	Noel	45	50
Emma	64	68	Wilma	70	64
Gibrine	49	54	Teshi	29	34

a Draw a scatter diagram with the GCSE results on the vertical axis.

b Comment on the strength of the correlation.

c Draw the line of best fit for this data.

d Estimate the GCSE results of a student who got 65 in the mid-year test.

e Comment on the likely accuracy of your estimate in part **d**.

4 Lyra read the following in the newspaper:
The New England Journal of Medicine reports that the number of Nobel prizes won by a country (adjusting for population) correlates well with per capita chocolate consumption.
Does this mean that eating chocolate may cause more people to win Nobel prizes? Give reasons for your answer.

HOMEWORK 3E

1 For the following data sets (A–C), one of the three averages is not representative. In each case state which average does not represent the data well and give a reason for your answer.

Data set A 6, 2, 5, 1, 5, 7, 2, 3, 8

Data set B 2, 0, 1, 3, 1, 6, 2, 9, 10, 3, 2, 2, 0

Data set C 21, 29, 30, 14, 5, 16, 3, 24, 17

2 A scatter plot of the age and shoe size of 11 boys is shown below.

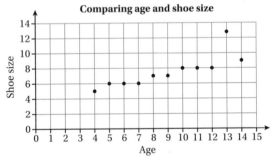

Comparing age and shoe size

a Comment on the correlation.

b Identify any outliers.

3 Silvie works as a waitress. She records her tips for the last eight shifts as shown below.

£10   £20   £10   £15   £30   £25   £10   £200

a Find the mean amount she is tipped.

b What is the range of tips?

c What is the median amount she received in tips?

d What is the median without the outlier?

e What is the mean without the outlier?

4 Pete has collected 50 pieces of data about people's spending habits.
He calculates that the median spend is £27.85.
The mean spend is £34.70.
The minimum amount spent is £3.11 and the maximum is £93.34.
Would you expect there to be any outliers in this data set?
Give a reason for your answer.

Age in years (a)	Frequency
$0 \leqslant a < 10$	13
$10 \leqslant a < 20$	28
$20 \leqslant a < 30$	39
$30 \leqslant a < 40$	46
$40 \leqslant a < 50$	48
$50 \leqslant a < 60$	31
$60 \leqslant a < 70$	19
Total	

Chapter 3 review

1 The mean of two consecutive numbers is 9.5
The mean of eight different numbers is 4.7
  a Calculate the total of the first two numbers.
  b What are these two numbers?
  c Calculate the mean of the ten numbers together.

2 Three suppliers sell specialised remote controllers for access systems.
A sample of 100 remote controllers is taken from each supplier and the working life of each controller is measured in weeks.
The following table shows the mean time and range for each supplier.

Supplier	Mean (weeks)	Range (weeks)
A	137	16
B	145	39
C	141	16

Which supplier would you recommend to someone who is looking to buy a remote controller? Why?

3 A box contains 50 plastic blocks of different volume as shown in the frequency table.

Volume (cm³)	2	3	4	5	6	7
Frequency	4	7	9	12	10	8

  a Find the mean volume of the blocks.
  b What volume is most common?
  c What is the median volume?

4 The ages of people who visited an art exhibition are recorded and organised in the grouped frequency table below.

  a Estimate the mean age of people attending the exhibition.
  b Into what age group did most visitors fall?
  c What is the median age of visitors to the exhibition?
  d Why can you not calculate an exact mean for this data set?

5 Study the scatter diagram and answer the questions.

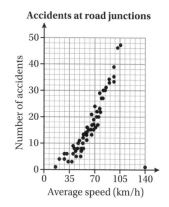

Accidents at road junctions

  a What does this diagram show?
  b What is the independent variable?
  c Copy the diagram and draw a line of best fit. Use your best fit line to predict:
    i the number accidents at the junction when the average speed of vehicles is 100 km/h
    ii what the average speed of vehicles is when there are fewer than 10 accidents.
  d Describe the correlation.
  e What does your answer to part **d** tell you about the relationship between speed and the number of accidents at a junction?
  f Comment on the outlier in this data set.

4 Properties of integers

Section 1: Types of numbers
HOMEWORK 4A

1 Write down the factors of the following numbers:
    a 24   **b** 673   **c** 81   **d** 53

2 Look at the numbers below.

4	15	8	25	7	16	12	9	6	23	36	96	27	3	1

Choose and write down the numbers in the list that are:
    a odd   **b** even
    c prime   **d** square
    e cube   **f** factors of 12
    g multiples of 4
    h common factors of 24 and 36
    i common multiples of 3 and 4.

Tip

Check you know the words for different types of number.

3 Write down:
    a the next four odd numbers after 313
    b the first four consecutive even numbers after 596
    c the square numbers between 40 and 100 inclusive
    d the factors of 43
    e four prime numbers between 30 and 50
    f the first five cube numbers
    g the first five multiples of 7
    h the factors of 48.

4 Say whether the results will be odd or even or could be either.
    a The product of two odd numbers
    b The sum of two odd numbers
    c The difference between two odd numbers
    d The square of an even number
    e The product of an odd and an even number
    f The cube of an even number

HOMEWORK 4B

1 Write these sets of numbers in order from smallest to biggest.
    a 476   736   458   634   453   4002
    b 1707   1770   1708   1870   1807
    c 345   543   453   354   534   435
    d 245   54   −245   −2004   205

2 What is the value of the 6 in each of these numbers?
    a 46   **b** 673   **c** 265   **d** 16 877
    e 64 475   **f** 1 654 782   **g** 6 035 784

3 What is the biggest and smallest number you can make with each set of digits?
Use each digit only once in each number.
    a 3, 0 and 7   **b** 6, 5, 1 and 9
    c 2, 3, 5, 0, 6 and 7
    d What is the difference between the biggest and smallest numbers in each question part?

4 Place the symbol =, < or > in each box to make each statement true.
    a 4 ☐ 5   **b** 3 + 5 ☐ 8
    c 9 ☐ 3 + 2   **d** 3 − 7 ☐ − 2

Section 2: Prime factors
HOMEWORK 4C

1 Identify the prime numbers in each set.
    a 10, 11, 12, 13, 14, 15, 16, 17, 18, 19, 20
    b 100, 101, 102, 103, 104, 105, 106, 107, 108, 109, 110

2 Express the following numbers as a product of their prime factors.
Use the method you prefer. Write your final answers using powers.
    a 48 **b** 75 **c** 81 **d** 315 **e** 560 **f** 2310
    g 735 **h** 1430 **i** 32 **j** 625 **k** 864

Tip

Remember each number has a unique set of prime factors.

3 A number is expressed as $13 \times 23 \times 7$
What is the number?

Section 3: Multiples and factors
HOMEWORK 4D

1 Find the LCM of the numbers below.
   a 12 and 16   **b** 15 and 20   **c** 12 and 20
   d 24 and 30   **e** 3, 4 and 6   **f** 5, 7 and 10

2 Find the HCF of the numbers below.
   a 18 and 24   **b** 36 and 48   **c** 27 and 45
   d 14 and 35   **e** 21 and 49   **f** 36 and 72

3 Find the LCM and the HCF of the following numbers by means of prime factors.
   a 28 and 98   **b** 75 and 20   **c** 144 and 24
   d 54 and 12   **e** 214 and 78

4 Amjad has two long pieces of timber.
One piece is 64 metres, the other is 80 metres.
He wants to cut the long pieces of timber into shorter pieces of equal length.
What is the longest he can make each piece?

Tip

Think carefully: is it the HCF or the LCM you need to find?

5 Two desert flowers have a life cycle of 11 years and 15 years respectively, when they are in bloom.
How many years are there between the occasions when they bloom at the same time?

6 Rochelle has 20 pieces of fruit and 55 sweets to share among the students in her class.
Each student gets the same number of pieces of fruit and each student gets the same number of sweets.
What is the largest possible number of students in her class?

Chapter 4 review

1 Is 243 a prime number? Write down how you worked out your answer.

2 Find the HCF and the LCM of 18 and 45 by listing the factors and multiples.

3 Express 675 as a product of prime factors, giving your final answer in power notation.

4 Find the HCF and the LCM of the following by prime factorisation.
   a 64 and 104   **b** 54 and 80

5 Working with fractions

Section 1: Equivalent fractions

Tip

Equivalent fractions are fractions with the same value, e.g. $\dfrac{1}{2} = \dfrac{2}{4}$

HOMEWORK 5A

1 Copy and complete each statement to make a pair of equivalent fractions.

   a $\dfrac{3}{4} = \dfrac{\square}{12}$ **b** $\dfrac{1}{3} = \dfrac{250}{\square}$ **c** $\dfrac{1}{4} = \dfrac{\square}{200}$ **d** $\dfrac{2}{3} = \dfrac{18}{\square}$

   e $\dfrac{3}{5} = \dfrac{36}{\square}$ **f** $\dfrac{\square}{24} = \dfrac{36}{16}$ **g** $\dfrac{7}{4} = \dfrac{28}{\square}$ **h** $\dfrac{20}{14} = \dfrac{50}{\square}$

2 Write each mixed number as an improper fraction.

   a $3\frac{1}{2}$ **b** $4\frac{2}{3}$ **c** $5\frac{4}{5}$ **d** $3\frac{2}{5}$

   e $7\frac{2}{7}$ **f** $5\frac{1}{6}$ **g** $6\frac{2}{9}$ **h** $11\frac{6}{7}$

3 Rewrite each fraction as an equivalent mixed number.

   a $\dfrac{13}{3}$ **b** $\dfrac{8}{3}$ **c** $\dfrac{11}{5}$ **d** $\dfrac{7}{5}$

   e $\dfrac{15}{13}$ **f** $\dfrac{15}{7}$ **g** $\dfrac{11}{3}$ **h** $\dfrac{24}{7}$

4 Which of the fractions in each of these pairs is the biggest?

a $\frac{2}{9}$ and $\frac{1}{4}$ b $\frac{2}{3}$ and $\frac{3}{5}$ c $\frac{3}{8}$ and $\frac{7}{15}$

d $\frac{2}{7}$ and $\frac{6}{21}$ e $\frac{3}{4}$ and $\frac{9}{15}$ f $\frac{20}{50}$ and $\frac{4}{10}$

g $\frac{8}{24}$ and $\frac{3}{9}$ h $\frac{12}{9}$ and $\frac{120}{99}$

> 💡 **Tip**
>
> Use equivalent fractions.

5 Reduce the following fractions to their simplest form.

a $\frac{3}{18}$ b $\frac{5}{20}$ c $\frac{50}{75}$ d $\frac{7}{21}$

e $\frac{8}{10}$ f $\frac{12}{28}$ g $\frac{48}{36}$ h $\frac{64}{96}$

6 Write the following fractions in order, smallest first:

$\frac{3}{5}$ $\frac{3}{8}$ $\frac{2}{7}$ $\frac{4}{9}$ $\frac{2}{3}$ $\frac{7}{20}$

Section 2: Using the four operations with fractions
HOMEWORK 5B

1 Work these out without using a calculator. You must show all your working.

a $\frac{3}{5} \times \frac{3}{8}$ b $\frac{5}{11} \times \frac{5}{7}$ c $\frac{3}{5} \times 45$ d $\frac{7}{9} \times \frac{7}{10}$

e $2\frac{4}{7} \times 3\frac{1}{2}$ f $5\frac{2}{9} \times 2\frac{1}{6}$ g $\frac{9}{20} \times 2\frac{7}{9}$ h $6\frac{1}{4} \times 3\frac{2}{3}$

> 💡 **Tip**
>
> Remember that any whole number can be expressed as a fraction over 1.

> 💡 **Tip**
>
> Change mixed numbers into improper fractions.

2 Work these out, without using a calculator, giving your answer in its simplest form.

a $\frac{1}{4} \times \frac{3}{7} \times \frac{5}{9}$ b $\frac{2}{5} \times \frac{5}{8} \times \frac{3}{10}$

c $\frac{1}{3} \times \frac{3}{4} \times \frac{6}{11}$ d $\frac{5}{9} \times \frac{3}{11} \times \frac{9}{10}$

e $\frac{4}{25} \times \frac{-3}{4} \times \frac{-5}{8}$ f $\frac{8}{15} \times \frac{10}{21} \times \frac{7}{12}$

3 Work these out, without using a calculator, giving your answer in its simplest form.

a $\frac{2}{5} + \frac{1}{2}$ b $\frac{5}{6} + \frac{3}{8}$ c $\frac{2}{3} - \frac{3}{5}$

d $12 - \frac{1}{6}$ e $\frac{11}{2} - \frac{7}{5}$ f $2\frac{3}{7} + 4\frac{1}{3}$

g $2\frac{2}{5} - 1\frac{2}{3}$ h $3\frac{7}{9} - 2\frac{5}{7}$

4 Work these out, without using a calculator, giving your answer in its simplest form.

a $\frac{1}{8} \div \frac{5}{9}$ b $\frac{2}{11} \div \frac{2}{7}$ c $\frac{4}{7} \div \frac{3}{8}$

d $\frac{-5}{11} \div \frac{-1}{3}$ e $\frac{3}{5} \div 2\frac{1}{4}$ f $2\frac{1}{4} \div \frac{3}{5}$

g $3\frac{1}{2} \div 1\frac{1}{3}$ h $1\frac{5}{6} \div 3\frac{3}{7}$

5 Work these out, without using a calculator, giving your answer in its simplest form.

a $3 + \frac{2}{5} \times \frac{2}{5}$ b $3\frac{3}{4} - \left(2\frac{1}{4} - \frac{4}{15}\right)$

c $\frac{5}{7} \times \left(\frac{1}{3} + 5 \div \frac{2}{5}\right) + 4 \times \frac{2}{7}$ d $5\frac{7}{8} + \left(7\frac{1}{3} - 5\frac{2}{9}\right)$

e $\frac{5}{7} \times \frac{1}{3} + \frac{3}{5} \times \frac{1}{3}$ f $\left(7 \div \frac{3}{7} - \frac{4}{9}\right) \times \frac{1}{5}$

HOMEWORK 5C

1 Shamso buys a 6 kg packet of mixed nuts and raisins, and she notices that $\frac{3}{8}$ of the contents are raisins.
How many kilograms of nuts were there?

2 Josh eats 12 bananas each week. Tara eats $2\frac{1}{4}$ times as many.
How many bananas do they eat in total?

3 $\frac{11}{24}$ of the people in a UK athletics team are from England, $\frac{3}{12}$ are from Wales, $\frac{1}{6}$ are from Scotland and the rest are from Northern Ireland.
a What fraction of the team are from Northern Ireland?
b Which country has the smallest number of team members?

4 There are $2\frac{1}{4}$ equally-sized cakes left over after a party. These are shared out equally amongst 6 people. What fraction does each person get?

5 A tanker contains $56\frac{1}{3}$ litres of juice. How many containers holding $\frac{5}{6}$ of a litre can be completely filled?

Section 3: Fractions of quantities
HOMEWORK 5D

1 Calculate:

a $\frac{5}{6}$ of 12   b $\frac{2}{9}$ of 45   c $\frac{3}{4}$ of 36

d $\frac{7}{12}$ of 144   e $\frac{4}{9}$ of 180   f $\frac{1}{8}$ of 96

g $\frac{1}{2}$ of $\frac{3}{7}$ h $\frac{2}{7}$ of $\frac{3}{14}$ i $\frac{4}{5}$ of $4\frac{1}{2}$

Tip

To find a fraction of a quantity, you need to divide by the denominator then multiply by the numerator.

2 Calculate the following quantities.

a $\frac{3}{4}$ of £48   b $\frac{3}{5}$ of £220

c $\frac{2}{5}$ of £45   d $\frac{2}{3}$ of £27

e $\frac{1}{2}$ of 7 potatoes   f $\frac{3}{4}$ of $2\frac{1}{2}$ cups of sugar

g $\frac{1}{4}$ of $4\frac{2}{3}$ cakes   h $\frac{2}{3}$ of 5 hours

i $\frac{1}{3}$ of $2\frac{3}{4}$ hours   j $\frac{3}{4}$ of 6 hours

3 Express the first quantity as a fraction of the second quantity. Give your answer in its simplest form.

a 6p in £1
b 25 cm of a 3 m length
c 15 mm of 30 cm
d 40 minutes in 8 hours
e 4 minutes per hour
f 175 m of a kilometre

Tip

Make sure both quantities are in the same units.

4 The floor area of a club room hall is 54 m². The dance floor is 3 m wide and 4 m long. What fraction of the floor area is the dance floor?

Chapter 5 review

1 Simplify:

a $\frac{12}{60}$ b $\frac{18}{108}$ c $4\frac{9}{36}$

2 Write each set of fractions in ascending order. Show all your working.

a $\frac{3}{4}, \frac{7}{9}, \frac{2}{3}, \frac{5}{6}$ b $\frac{14}{5}, \frac{11}{4}, 2\frac{1}{2}, 2\frac{3}{10}$

3 Evaluate:

a $\frac{1}{4} + \frac{3}{7}$ b $\frac{4}{7} \times \frac{3}{5}$

c $\frac{5}{9} \div \frac{3}{7}$ d $4\frac{2}{9} + 1\frac{1}{6}$

e $6\frac{3}{10} - 3\frac{2}{5}$ f $\frac{3}{7}$ of $\frac{2}{3}$

g $\frac{2}{9} \times \frac{2}{11} \times 3$ h $96 \div \frac{3}{8}$

i $\frac{1}{6}$ of $5\frac{2}{7}$

4 Simplify:

a $\left(\frac{5}{8} \div \frac{15}{4}\right) + \left(\frac{4}{9} \times \frac{3}{8}\right)$

b $3\frac{3}{4} \times \left(\frac{5}{8} + \frac{5}{6}\right)$

5 Lisa has $15\frac{1}{2}$ litres of water. How many bottles containing $\frac{3}{4}$ litre can she fill?

6 At a Fun Day there are 5 litres of ice cream to be sold in cones. If each cone has at least $\frac{2}{25}$ of a litre of ice cream, what is the maximum number of cones that can be made?

6 Working with decimals

Section 1: Review of decimals and fractions

HOMEWORK 6A

1 Write the following decimals as fractions in their simplest form.

   a 0.8   b 0.64   c 2.25

   d 0.979   e 0.0125   f 0.005

   g 0.66   h 0.435

2 Convert the following fractions to decimals without using a calculator.

   a $\dfrac{2}{5}$ b $\dfrac{7}{10}$ c $\dfrac{11}{200}$

   d $\dfrac{3}{25}$ e $\dfrac{9}{20}$ f $\dfrac{7}{50}$

   g $\dfrac{3}{250}$ h $\dfrac{3}{8}$

3 Convert the following fractions to decimals using a calculator.

   a $\dfrac{1}{3}$ b $\dfrac{2}{9}$ c $\dfrac{5}{12}$

   d $\dfrac{7}{18}$ e $\dfrac{5}{24}$ f $\dfrac{10}{33}$

   g What do you notice about the denominator in each parts **a** to **f**?

   h Can you make a general rule from this?

4 Arrange the following in ascending order.

   $6\frac{3}{10}$, 6.21, $7\frac{3}{5}$, 5.98, 3.07

5 Arrange the following in ascending order.

   a 24.3, 24.72, 24.07, 24.89, 24.009

   b 0.53, 0.503, 0.524, 0.058, 0.505, 0.5

6 Copy each pair of numbers and use <, = or > to make each statement true.

   a $\dfrac{1}{2}\ \square\ 0.499$ b $\dfrac{2}{5}\ \square\ 0.25$

   c $0.867\ \square\ 0.876$ d $\dfrac{5}{8}\ \square\ 0.7$

   e $\dfrac{8}{32}\ \square\ 0.25$

7 The dimensions of three cars are given in the table below.

Car	Length (m)	Width (m)	Height (m)
Alfa Romeo Guilietta	4.351	1.798	1.465
BMW Z4	4.239	1.79	1.291
Jaguar F-type	4.47	1.923	1.308

   a Write the cars in order of length, shortest first.

   b Write the cars in descending order of width.

   c Write the cars in ascending order of height.

Section 2: Calculating with decimals

HOMEWORK 6B

1 A bottle of olive oil contains 0.475 litres and costs £3.55.

   a Can you buy three bottles for £10?

   b What is the price of the olive oil per litre?

   c How many bottles would you need to buy to have at least 2 litres of olive oil?

   d At a warehouse olive oil is sold in 20 litre drums. How many bottles could you completely fill from such a drum?

   e A recipe for a salad dressing uses 15 ml of olive oil. How many portions of salad dressing could be made with one bottle?

HOMEWORK 6C

1 A series of rectangles are created using different side lengths.

   Calculate the area of each rectangle.

   a 4.55 m × 2.3 m

   b 1.05 cm × 6.9 cm

   c 35.8 cm × 12.05 cm

   d 45.15 m × 84.21 m

HOMEWORK 6D

1 Estimate then calculate. Show your working.
  a $0.7 + 0.35$ **b** $13.7 - 2.9$ **c** $1.2 + 0.4$
  d $18.31 - 4.96$ **e** 3.53×2.4 **f** 8.99×5.2

2 Work these out without using a calculator.
  a $13.8 + 45.6 + 3.97$
  b $34.65 + 5.08 + 2.8$
  c $65.87 - 8.6$
  d $45.93 - 17.69$
  e $43.9 + 9.24 - 12.16$
  f 0.87×100
  g 9.56×200
  h 4.35×7.53
  i $0.564 \div 8$
  j $7.2 \div 0.8$
  k $9.456 \div 0.4$
  l $6.84 \div 3.2$

3 The table below shows the last six women's world record times in 50 m freestyle swimming.

Record holder	Time (s)
Jill Sterkel	26.32
Kelly Asplund	26.53
Cynthia Woodhead	26.61
Anne Jardin	26.74
Johanna Malloy	26.95
Kornelia Ender	26.99

  a What is the time difference between the fastest and slowest in the table?
  b What is the biggest difference in the world record times in the table?
  c Calculate the average speed of Jill Sturkel in metres per second on her record breaking swim. Give your answer to one decimal place.

4 Marita eats a bowl of porridge every morning. She calculates that if she eats the same quantity every day for a week she will take in 14.49 g of fat, 139.16 g of carbohydrate and 35.49 g of protein. How much of each will she eat in a single serving?

HOMEWORK 6E

1 Sandita has £117.50 in her pocket. She buys three tops that cost £27.99 each. How much money will she have left?

2 The odometer in Jules' car reads 129 985.3 km when he leaves Norwich and 130 128.7 when he arrives in London. How far did he travel?

3 Jim has 2800 wooden stakes which are 0.6 m long. If he laid them end to end in a straight line, how long would the line be?

4 Juanita fills her car with 18.9 litres of petrol at £1.37 per litre.
  a How much will this cost?
  b When she gets to the checkout she finds a voucher for 5 pence off per litre. What is the total amount she pays?

Chapter 6 review

1 Arrange each set of numbers in ascending order.
  a $6.5, 6.05, 6.55, 6.501, 6.505$
  b $\dfrac{2}{3}, 0.67, 0.607, 0.61, 0.66, \dfrac{5}{8}$

2 Convert these fractions to decimals and insert $<$, $=$ or $>$ to compare the fractions.
  a $\dfrac{5}{8} \square \dfrac{3}{4}$ **b** $\dfrac{7}{10} \square \dfrac{13}{20}$
  c $\dfrac{9}{13} \square \dfrac{11}{15}$ **d** $\dfrac{8}{9} \square \dfrac{7}{8}$

3 Write each as a fraction in its simplest terms.
  a 0.46 **b** 0.72 **c** 0.08 **d** 0.075

4 **a** Increase $\dfrac{1}{5}$ by 3.4
  b Reduce 89.65 by $\dfrac{1}{4}$ of 32.8
  c Divide 6 by 0.75
  d Multiply 0.7 by 0.6

5 **a** Add 46.86 and 34.08
  b Subtract 4.846 from 8.56
  c Multiply 7.84 by 200
  d Divide 29.56 by 100
  e Multiply 3.19 by 0.8
  f Simplify $\dfrac{76.8}{3.2}$

6 Gerry and Judith have £24 each. Gerry spends 0.425 of his money and Judith spends $\dfrac{9}{20}$ of hers.
  a Who has most money left?
  b How much more do they have?

7 Basic algebra

Section 1: Algebraic notation
HOMEWORK 7A

1 Which of the following are terms and which are expressions?
a $3x$ b $4x$ c $6y$ d x e $3x + 4y$ f $3x^2$

2 Write an expression for the following statements using the conventions for algebra.
a A number x is multiplied by 4 and has 3 added to it
b A number x is multiplied by 2 and added to y multiplied by 5
c A number x is squared and 7 is subtracted from it. This is then multiplied by 3
d A number x is cubed and added to a number y squared, and this is all divided by 2
e A number x has 2 subtracted from it and the result is divided by 3

Tip

Remember letters represent numbers.

3 Match each statement to its correct algebraic expression.

A number x is multiplied by 2 and has 7 added to it. The result is divided by 3	$3x - 7$
A number x is squared, then multiplied by 3, and added to a number y multiplied by 7	$x^2 + 3x$
A number x is multiplied by 3 and has 7 taken from the result.	$3x^2 + 7y$
A number x is added to a number y, and the result is multiplied by 3	$(2x + 7) \div 3$
A number x is squared, and then added to the original number multiplied by 3	$3(x + y)$

4 Simplify these expressions.
a $5 \times 2x$ b $3a \times 2$ c $x \times (-5)$
d $3x \times 6y$ e $3a \times 5b$ f $-3p \times 3q$

g $16x \div 4$ h $25y \div 5$ i $32a^2 \div 4$
j $6 \times 10p \div 20$ k $27x \div (3 \times 3)$ l $24y \div (4 \times 2)$

5 Write an expression to represent the area of each of these rectangles.

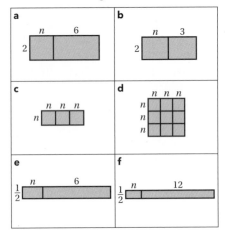

6 I think of a number.
I double the number.
I add 4 to the result.
I multiply the result by three.
I divide the result by two.
I divide the result by three.
If I take away the first number I thought of, the answer is always 2.
Write down why this is the case.

7 A woman is x years old.
a How old was she 5 years ago?
b How old will she be in 12 years time?
b Her mother is twice her age. How old is her mother?
d Her daughter is half her age. How old is her daughter?

HOMEWORK 7B

1 Given that $x = 4$ and $y = 7$, evaluate these expressions.
a $3x + 2y$ b $4x - 2y$ c $8y - 2x$
d $y + 3x$ e $3xy$ f $\frac{1}{2}xy$
g $5x - 2y$ h $y - 2x$

2 Find the value of each expression when $a = -3$ and $b = 4$

a $-3ab + 4$ **b** $-3ab - 8$ **c** $\dfrac{12}{b}$

d $\dfrac{12}{a}$ **e** $\dfrac{a}{3} + \dfrac{-4}{b}$ **f** $a + 2b - 6$

Section 2: Simplifying expressions
HOMEWORK 7C

1 Which of the following pairs are like terms? Collect the like terms where possible.

a $10x$ and $4a$ **b** $8b$ and $-3b$

c $9m$ and $6n$ **d** $5p$ and $-7r$

e $-8xy$ and $-5y$ **f** $10x^2$ and $5x^2$

g $7x^2$ and $-7x^2$ **h** $6x^2$ and $-2x$

i $3a^2bc$ and $4a^2bc^2$

Tip

You cannot add $3a$ to $4b$ unless you know what a and b are!

2 Write these expressions in their simplest form by collecting like terms.

a $3a + 6b - 7a + 4b$

b $6a + 9b - 5a - 8b$

c $4ab + 5b^2 + 7ab - 7b^2$

d $4m^2 - mn^2 + mn^2 + 6mn$

e $8cd^3 - 24cd^3 + 5cd^3$

f $4st^2 - 4s^2t + 7s^2t + 5st^2$

3 Copy and complete.

a $4a + \boxed{} = 10a$

b $7b - \boxed{} = 6b$

c $12mn + \boxed{} = 15mn$

d $17pq + \boxed{} = 8pq$

e $9x^2 - \boxed{} = 12x^2$

f $8m^2 - \boxed{} = -m^2$

g $6ab - \boxed{} = -2ab$

4 Copy and complete.

a $6a \times \boxed{} = 18a$

b $7b \times \boxed{} = 14b$

c $4a \times \boxed{} = 12ab$

d $7m \times \boxed{} = 28mn$

e $-4b \times \boxed{} = 12b^2$

f $6m \times \boxed{} = 12m^2n$

5 Simplify:

a $\dfrac{6x}{2}$ **b** $\dfrac{4a}{12}$

c $\dfrac{-16m}{24}$ **d** $\dfrac{14x^2}{21}$

e $\dfrac{9ab}{a}$ **f** $\dfrac{4xy}{12xy}$

Section 3: Expanding brackets
HOMEWORK 7D

1 Expand the brackets and collect any like terms to simplify the following.

a $3(a + 4) - 9$

b $4(a - 3) + 2$

c $6(b + 4) - 10$

d $4(e - 6) + 17$

e $3(x - 7) - 4$

f $3a(2a + 5) + 8a$

g $3b(4b - 7) - 6b$

h $3a(4a + 7) + 5a^2$

i $5b(4b - 5) - 9b^2$

Tip

Multiply everything inside the bracket by the number or number and letter outside the bracket.

2 Expand and collect like terms for each expression.

a $3(x + 2) + 4(x + 5)$

b $3(4a - 1) + 4(3a - 2)$

c $4(c + 6) - 3(c + 7)$

d $4(a - 3) - 3(a + 4)$

e $x(x - 5) + 2(x - 7)$

f $5q(q + 3) - 5(q + 2)$

g $2y(y + 5) - y(2y + 3)$

h $2x(x - 5) + x(x - 3)$

3 The expression in each box is equal to the sum of the expressions in the two boxes below it. Find the missing expressions for the empty boxes.

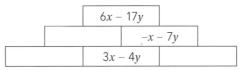

17

Section 4: Factorising expressions
HOMEWORK 7E

1. State which of the following are expressions, identities or equations.
   a $3(a + b) = 3a + 3b$　　b $x + y = y + x$
   c $xy^2 + x^2$　　d $3a + 5$
   e $4a + 7b = 22$　　f $x(x + 1) = x^2 + x$

Section 5: Solving problems using algebra
HOMEWORK 7F

1. a Copy and complete this magic square, filling in the missing expressions.

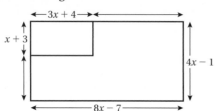

$3n + 8$	$3n - 13$	$3n + 2$
	$3n - 1$	

   b Write an expression for the magic number.

2. A large rectangle as shown below contains a smaller rectangle.

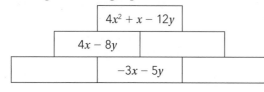

   a Write an expression for each of missing lengths.
   b Write an expression for the perimeter of the small rectangle.
   c Write an expression for the perimeter of the large rectangle.
   d Write an expression for the perimeter of the compound shape formed by removing the small rectangle from the large rectangle.

3. Copy and complete the pyramid below by finding the missing expressions.

	$4x^2 + x - 12y$	

$4x - 8y$	

	$-3x - 5y$	

4. Which of the following in this table are always true or sometimes true?
   If the answer is sometimes, state when it is true.

	Always true	Sometimes true when…	Never true
$x + 4 = 7$			
$3x - 4 = 4 - 3x$			
$2x - 4 = 2y - 4$			
$3(n - 4) = 3n - 12$			
$x^2 + 3x + 4 = 4 + x(x + 3)$			

Chapter 7 review

1. The expression $6(x + 3) - 4(x - 3)$ simplifies to $a(x + b)$. Work out the values of a and b.

2. Simplify the following expressions fully by collecting like terms where possible.
   a $4(x + 3) + 8x - 5x + 12 + 7x$
   b $4(x - 3) + 3(x - 4)$
   c $2x(x - 3) + 3x - x^2$
   d $21x^3 \div 3x + 6x^3 \div x$
   e $2x(3x + 8) - 8x$
   f $4a(4a - 3) - 4b$
   g $4a(5a - 6) + 3a^2$
   h $3x(4x - 5) - 5x^2$

3. Which of these are identities?
   a $6x + 4 = 3x + 2$
   b $5xy + 3 = 3 + 5xy$
   c $x^2 = 2x$
   d $x(y + 7) = xy + 7x$

4. Dots are arranged to represent the perimeter of a square, as in the diagram below:

   If n is the number of dots on a side, show that the total number of dots can be expressed as $4(n - 1)$, $4(n - 2) + 4$ and $2(n - 2) + 2n$.

8 Properties of polygons and 3D objects

Section 1: Types of shapes
HOMEWORK 8A

1 What is the correct mathematical name for each of the following shapes?
  a A plane shape with four sides
  b A polygon with six equal sides
  c A polygon with five vertices and five equal internal angles
  d A plane shape with ten equal sides and ten equal internal angles

Tip
Learn the names of shapes and be clear which are regular and which are irregular.

2 What are the names of the following shapes in the diagrams (**a–d**) below?

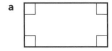
a

b

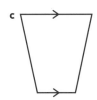
c

d

3 Name each shape given the following properties.
  a A four-sided shape with two pairs of equal and opposite sides but no right angles
  b A four-sided shape with only one pair of parallel sides
  c A triangle with two equal angles
  d A triangle with all sides and angles equal
  e A four-sided shape with two pairs of equal and adjacent sides

Tip
It is a good idea to learn the properties of quadrilaterals.

4 Write down the mathematical name for each of the following shapes.
  a A plane shape with four equal sides
  b A polygon with eight equal sides
  c A polygon with three sides, two of which are equal

5 Give an example of where you might see the following shapes in real life.
  a A regular hexagon
  b A cuboid
  c An equilateral triangle

HOMEWORK 8B

1 Look at the diagram below and state whether the following statements are true or false.

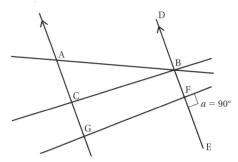
$a = 90°$

  a AG is parallel to DE.
  b ABC is an isosceles triangle.
  c DE is perpendicular to BC.
  d AG is perpendicular to GF.
  e AB is perpendicular to AG.
  f AB and GF are parallel.

2 Draw and correctly label a sketch of each of the following shapes.
  a Triangle ABC with a right angle at A and AB = AC
  b A quadrilateral PQRS with two pairs of opposite equal angles, none of which are right angles, and two pairs of opposite equal sides
  c Quadrilateral ABCD where AB is parallel to CD and the angle ABC is a right angle

Section 2: Symmetry
HOMEWORK 8C

1 How many lines of symmetry do these shapes have?
  a A square
  b A kite
  c A regular hexagon
  d Equilateral triangle

> 💡 **Tip**
>
> Line symmetry cuts a shape in half so that one side is a mirror image of the other.

2 Give an example of a shape which has the following order of rotational symmetry.
  a 2   b 3   c 4

3 Which of the following letters have rotational symmetry?

  N I C K

> 💡 **Tip**
>
> Rotational symmetry is when the shape looks exactly the same after a rotation.

4 What is the order of rotational symmetry for each of the images (a–c) shown below?

  a    b

c

Section 3: Triangles
HOMEWORK 8D

1 What type of triangle do you see in this coat hanger? Write down how you decided without measuring.

> 💡 **Tip**
>
> Learn the properties of the different types of triangle.

2 a What type of triangle is shown below?
  b Give a reason why this triangle cannot be isosceles.

3 State whether the following triangles are possible. How did you decide?
  a Side lengths 6 cm, 8 cm, 10 cm
  b Side lengths 12 cm, 4 cm, 5 cm
  c Side lengths 7 cm, 11 cm, 5 cm
  d Side lengths 35 cm, 45 cm, 80 cm

4 Two angles in a triangle are 27° and 126°.
  a What is the size of the third angle?
  b What type of triangle is this?

5 Look at the diagram below and work out the following angles.

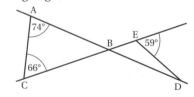

  a Angle ABC   b Angle BED   c Angle BDE

Tip

Use the properties of triangles and angles to answer this question.

6 An isosceles triangle PQR with PQ = QR has a perimeter of 80 cm.
Find the length of PQ if:
a PR = 24 cm
b PR = 53 cm

Section 4: Quadrilaterals
HOMEWORK 8E

1 Identify the quadrilateral from the description. Please note that there may be more than one correct answer.
a All sides are equal.
b Diagonals cross at right angles.
c One pair of sides is parallel.
d Two pairs of sides are parallel and equal in length.

2 Molly says that all four-sided shapes have at least one pair of equal or parallel sides.
Is she right?

3 A regular kite ABCD has angle ABC = 43° and the opposite angle ADC = 75°.
What size are the other two angles?

4 One pair of triangles has the angles 36°, 54° and 90°, whilst another pair has the angles 24°, 66° and 90°. The length of the shortest side in each of the four triangles is the same.
Imagine all four triangles placed together so that the right angles meet at the same point.
a What shape has been formed?
b What are the sizes of the four angles of this new shape?

5 a Write down the names of all the quadrilaterals.
b Which quadrilaterals have at least two equal sides?
c Which quadrilaterals have at least one pair of parallel sides?
d Which quadrilaterals have no rotational symmetry?

Section 5: Properties of 3D objects
HOMEWORK 8F

1 Sketch an example of each of the following solids.
a A cylinder
b A cuboid
c A hexagonal prism
d A square-based pyramid

Tip

Try to visualise the solid.

2 What is the difference between a square and a cube?

3 Compare a cuboid and a rectangular-based pyramid. How are they similar? How are they different?

4 Name a solid that has four flat faces.

5 Which solids fit the following descriptions?
a 6 vertices, 9 edges and 5 faces
b 5 faces, 5 vertices and 8 edges
c 24 edges, 16 vertices and 10 faces

Chapter 8 review

1 True or false?
a A triangle with two equal angles is called isosceles.
b A cuboid has 8 vertices, 6 faces and 10 edges.
c A pair of lines that meet at precisely 90° are described as being perpendicular.
d Every square is a rhombus.
e Every rectangle is a parallelogram.
f Every square is a rectangle.

2 Describe all the symmetrical features of a rectangle.

3 Find the missing angles in the trapezium shown below.

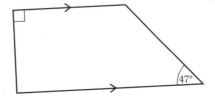

9 Angles

Section 1: Angle facts
HOMEWORK 9A

> **Tip**
>
> Remember: angles at a point = 360°,
> vertically opposite angles are equal,
> angles on a straight line = 180°.

1. Find the value of the missing angle x in each diagram (**a–c**) shown below.

   a   **b**   **c**

2. Jenny has drawn and labelled the diagram shown below.

   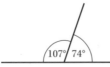

   What is wrong with Jenny's diagram?

3. What is the value of x in the diagram below?

4. In the diagram below, AB and CD are straight lines intersecting at E. Which angles are equal?

   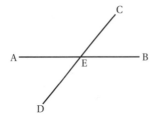

5. In the diagram at the top of the next column PQ and RS are straight lines that meet at T. UT is the bisector of the angle RTQ. Calculate the angles listed and give reasons for your answers.

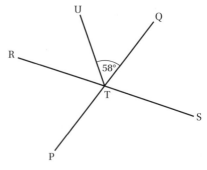

a Angle RTU   **b** Angle RTS
c Angle RTP   **d** Angle QTS
e Angle STP

> **Tip**
>
> Remember 'bisect' means to 'cut into two equal halves'.

Section 2: Parallel lines and angles
HOMEWORK 9B

1. Draw and label two parallel lines and a transversal to show the following angles.

> **Tip**
>
> A transversal is a line that crosses at least two other lines.

   a A pair of alternate angles
   b A pair of corresponding angles
   c A pair of co-interior angles

> **Tip**
>
> When formed between parallel lines, corresponding angles are equal, alternate angles are equal and co-interior angles are supplementary (add up to 180°).

2 In the diagram below, the lines AB and CD are parallel, as are AC and BD. The angle CAB = 66°

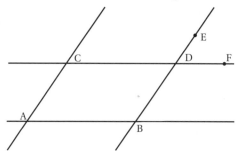

a Write down the size of angle ACD. Give a reason for your answer.
b Write down the size of angle EDF. Give a reason for your answer.
c Write down the size of angle ABD. Give a reason for your answer.
d Name one other angle that is equal to CAB.
e What shape is ACDB? Give a reason for your answer.

3 Use the diagram below to find the following angles. Give reasons for your answers.

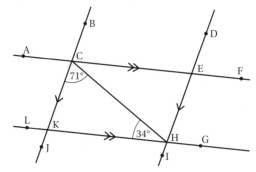

a Angle ECH   b Angle ACB   c Angle ACK
d Angle IHG   e Angle CEH   f Angle DEF

Section 3: Angles in triangles
HOMEWORK 9C

1 A triangle has an angle of 54° and another of 74°. What is the size of the third angle in the triangle?

Tip
Angles in a triangle = 180°.

2 An isosceles triangle has two equal angles of 37°. What is the size of the third angle in the triangle?

3 The triangle ABC has an interior angle at A of 52°. The exterior angle formed by a line through BC at C = 121°. What is the size of the interior angle at B?

Tip
The exterior angle of any triangle is equal to the sum of the opposite interior angles.

4 In the triangle DEF, the interior angle at D is a right angle.

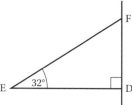

a What is the size of the exterior angle shown at F?
b If the line DE were extended beyond E, what would be the size of the exterior angle formed at E?

5 In the diagram below, the lines AB, CD and EF are parallel. The distance HJ = HG

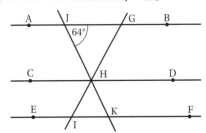

a Find the following angles, giving reasons for your answers.
 i Angle HKI
 ii Angle HIK
 iii Angle IHK
 iv Angle JHD
 v Angle GHD
b What sort of triangle is GHJ?
c Give a reason for your answer.

Section 4: Angles in polygons
HOMEWORK 9D

1. What is the exterior angle at any vertex in the following shapes?
   a An equilateral triangle   b A square
   c A regular hexagon

2. What is the size of an interior angle at any vertex in the following shapes?
   a A regular pentagon
   b A regular octagon
   c A regular decagon
   d Any regular polygon with n sides

3. Calculate the sum of interior angles of a polygon with:
   a 11 sides   b 15 side   c 30 sides.

4. Calculate the sum of the exterior angles for:
   a a 12-sided shape   b a 250-sided shape.

5. The diagram below shows a regular pentagon ABCDE.

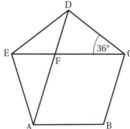

   a Calculate:
      i Angle DFE   ii Angle EFA   iii Angle FAB
   b What shape is ABCF?
   c Give a reason for your answer.
   d What shape is AEF?
   e Give a reason for your answer.

HOMEWORK 9E

1. In a regular hexagon, what is the size of each interior angle?

2. Calculate the sum of the interior angles in a polygon with:
   a 10 sides   b 15 sides   c 36 sides.

3. A regular polygon has 12 sides. Find:
   a the sum of the interior angles
   b the sum of the exterior angles
   c the size of an interior angle
   d the size of an exterior angle.

4. A regular polygon has an interior angle which is half the size of the exterior angle.
   a What is the size of each interior angle?
   b What is the size of each exterior angle?
   c What is the name of the shape?

5. A pentagon has three angles that add up to 270°. If the other two angles are equal, what size is each of these angles?

Chapter 9 review

1. Use the diagram below to find the following angles. Give reasons for your answers.

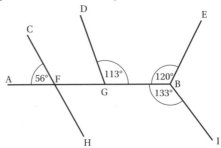

   a Angle EBI   b Angle DGF
   c Angle GFH   d Angle AFH

2. The diagram below, shows two pairs of parallel lines. Calculate the marked angles, giving reasons for your answers.

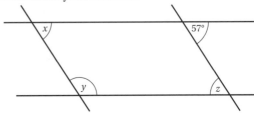

3. One of the two equal angles in an isosceles triangle is 39°. What are the sizes of the other two angles?

4. The triangle ABC has an exterior angle of 34° at B and an interior angle of 19° at A. What is the size of the interior angle at C?

5. A 20-sided polygon is known as an icosagon.
   a What is the size of an interior angle of a regular icosagon?
   b What is the sum of the interior angles of an icosagon?
   c What is the size of an exterior angle in a regular icosagon?
   d What is the sum of the exterior angles in an icosagon?

10 Perimeter

Section 1: Perimeter of simple and composite shapes

HOMEWORK 10A

1 Calculate the perimeter of each of the shapes (**a–f**) below.

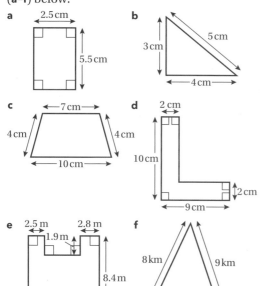

2 Find the perimeter of each of the shapes (**a–f**) below.

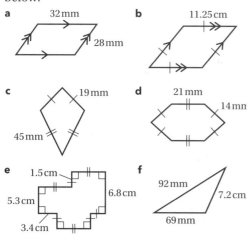

3 Work out the perimeter of each shape.
   a An equilateral triangle with sides of length 12.6 cm
   b A square with sides of length $2x$ cm
   c A rectangle which is 132 mm long and 6.5 cm wide

4 Find the cost of fencing a rectangular plot 45 m long and 37 m wide if the fencing costs £23.80 per metre. Leave 2.5 m unfenced for the gate.

5 A rectangular field has a perimeter of 326 m. The width is at least 60 m and the length is at least 75 m. Suggest five possible sets of dimensions for the field.

6 Six square tiles are arranged in a row as shown in the diagram. The perimeter of the rectangle formed by the tiles is 315 cm.
   a What is the length of the sides of the square tiles?
   b If the same tiles were rearranged as shown, what would the perimeter of the rectangle be then?

HOMEWORK 10B

1 The perimeters of the shapes (**a–h**) in the diagrams below are given. For each shape, find the value of x.

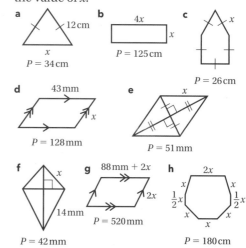

25

2 Each of the shapes (**a–h**) below has a perimeter of 30 cm. Work out the length of the unknown side or sides in each shape. Dimensions are in cm.

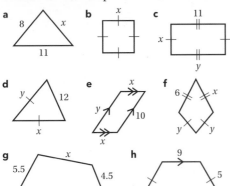

3 An isosceles triangle has a perimeter of 28 cm. The equal sides are x m long and the third side is 100 mm long. What is the length of each equal side?

Tip

Make sure all measurements are in the same units before you do any calculations.

4 A rectangle is three times as long as it is wide. If it has a perimeter of 480 mm, what are the dimensions of the sides?

Section 2: Circumference of a circle
HOMEWORK 10C

Tip

For circle questions use the π button on your calculator unless told otherwise.

Give all your answers to three significant figures.

1 Find the perimeter of each of the shapes (**a–f**) shown below.

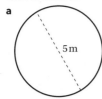

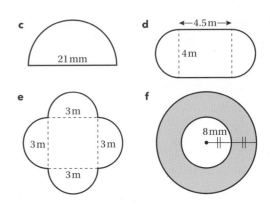

2 Calculate the circumference of a circle with diameter:

a 21 m   **b** 4.08 cm
c 1.8 m   **d** 2.5 cm
e 14.24 m   **f** 88 cm
g 10 m

3 The rim of a bicycle wheel has a radius of 31.5 cm.
  a What is the circumference of the rim?
  b The tyre that goes onto the rim is 3.5 cm thick. Calculate the circumference of the wheel when the tyre is fitted to it.

4 How much string would you need to form a circular loop with a diameter of 28 cm?

5 What is the radius of a circle of circumference:
  a 81 cm?   **b** 31.5 cm?   **c** 220 cm?

HOMEWORK 10D

1 Find the perimeter of the shapes (**a–e**) below. Give your answers to three significant figures.

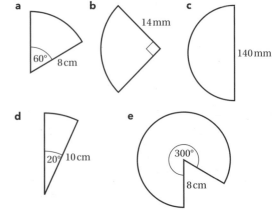

2 Work out the length of the arc marked x in each of the circles (**a-d**) below.

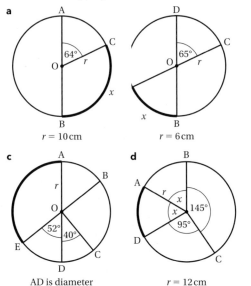

a

$r = 10\,cm$

$r = 6\,cm$

c

AD is diameter
$r = 5\,cm$

d

$r = 12\,cm$

3 Nicky is stuck in traffic. She has driven 23 m from point A to point B around a roundabout of radius 14 m as shown in the diagram.

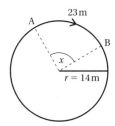

a Work out the circumference of the roundabout.

b What is the size of angle x?

Section 3: Problems involving perimeter and circumference
HOMEWORK 10E

1 Work out which shaded shape (A or B) has the greater perimeter and say how much greater it is.

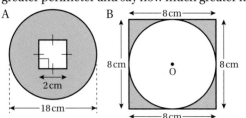

2 The diagram below shows a silver pendant with a gold ring around it.

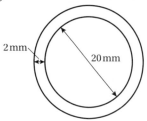

Calculate, to one decimal place, the circumference of:
a the inner silver pendant
b the outer gold ring.

3 Find the distance around the track shown below.

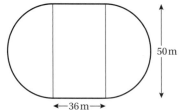

4 Look at the diagram of a dartboard carefully. The dartboard has a diameter of 41 cm. The divisions between numbers and sections are outlined in thin metal wire (indicated by the black lines on this diagram). Use the given dimensions to work out the total length of wire on this dartboard. Show all your calculations.

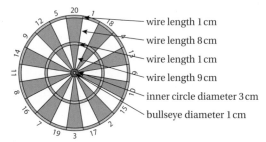

wire length 1 cm
wire length 8 cm
wire length 1 cm
wire length 9 cm
inner circle diameter 3 cm
bullseye diameter 1 cm

Chapter 10 review

1 Calculate the perimeter of each of the shapes (**a-g**).

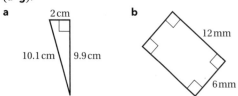

a

2 cm
10.1 cm 9.9 cm

b

12 mm
6 mm

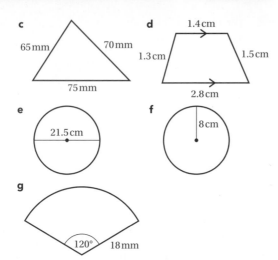

c 65 mm, 70 mm, 75 mm

d 1.4 cm, 1.3 cm, 1.5 cm, 2.8 cm

e 21.5 cm

f 8 cm

g 120°, 18 mm

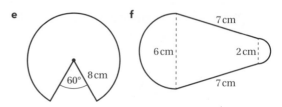

e 60°, 8 cm

f 7 cm, 6 cm, 2 cm, 7 cm

3. A pizza company advertises the following pizza sizes as shown in the diagram below.

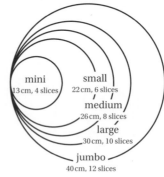

mini
13 cm, 4 slices

small
22 cm, 6 slices

medium
26 cm, 8 slices

large
30 cm, 10 slices

jumbo
40 cm, 12 slices

a Calculate the circumference of each pizza size offered.

b The pizzas are cut into different numbers of slices. Assuming each slice of a particular pizza is the same size, draw a diagram to show the dimensions of one slice of each pizza size. Include the arc lengths and the size of the angle at the centre.

c Suggest suitable dimensions for the smallest possible rectangular box to package one slice of each pizza size.

2. Work out the perimeter of each of the shapes (**a–f**) below.

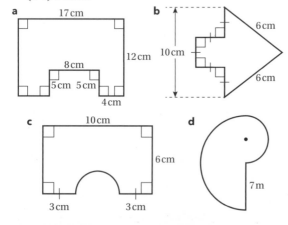

a 17 cm, 8 cm, 5 cm, 5 cm, 4 cm, 12 cm

b 6 cm, 10 cm, 6 cm

c 10 cm, 6 cm, 3 cm, 3 cm

d 7 m

11 Area

Section 1: Area of polygons
HOMEWORK 11A

1. Write a formula for finding the area of shapes (**a–c**) shown below.

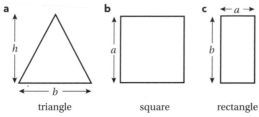

a triangle (h, b)

b square (a)

c rectangle (a, b)

2. Work out the area of each of the triangles and kites (**a–i**) shown below.

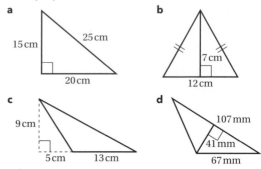

a 15 cm, 25 cm, 20 cm

b 7 cm, 12 cm

c 9 cm, 5 cm, 13 cm

d 107 mm, 41 mm, 67 mm

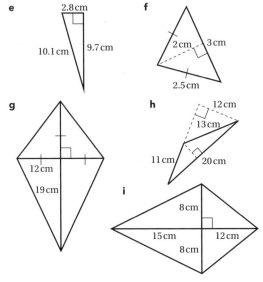

e 2.8 cm 9.7 cm 10.1 cm

f 2 cm 3 cm 2.5 cm

g 12 cm 19 cm

h 12 cm 13 cm 11 cm 20 cm

i 8 cm 15 cm 12 cm 8 cm

3 A triangle has a base of 9 cm and a height of 5 cm, what is its area?

4 A triangle of area 80 cm² has a base of length 15 cm. What is its height?

5 A triangular sail has a height of 5.65 m and an area of 68.93 m². What is the length of its base?

6 The two symmetrical arrow designs shown below (A and B) are used as markings in a sports ground. Work out the area of each arrow.

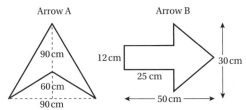

Arrow A   Arrow B

90 cm   12 cm
60 cm   25 cm   30 cm
90 cm   50 cm

7 The arrows in the previous question are painted white. One tin of white paint covers an area of 0.8 m². Work out how much paint you would need to paint:
a 35 arrows of design A
b 20 arrows of design B
c 100 arrows of design A and 125 arrows of design B.

Tip

How to convert units of area is covered in Student Book Chapter 11. Read that through again if you have forgotten how to do this.

HOMEWORK 11B

1 Write a formula for working out the area of each of the following shapes (**a–d**).

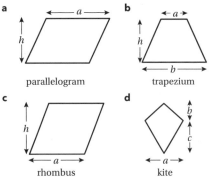

a
a
h
parallelogram

b
a
h
b
trapezium

c
h
a
rhombus

d
b
c
a
kite

2 Work out the area of each of the shapes (**a–i**) below. Pay attention to the units.

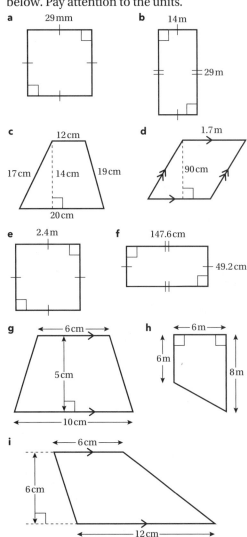

a 29 mm

b 14 m
29 m

c 12 cm
17 cm   14 cm   19 cm
20 cm

d 1.7 m
90 cm

e 2.4 m

f 147.6 cm
49.2 cm

g 6 cm
5 cm
10 cm

h 6 m
6 m
8 m

i 6 cm
6 cm
12 cm

3 Calculate the area of each of the following shapes **a–c**. Give your answers to two decimal places.
  a A square of side 12.6 cm.
  b A rectangle with sides of 8.5 m and 12.2 m.
  c A trapezium of height 12 cm and parallel sides of 8.5 cm and 11.8 cm.

4 A rhombus has an area of 5600 mm² and sides of length 8 cm. What is its perpendicular height?

Section 2: Area of circles and sectors
HOMEWORK 11C

1 Find the area of each of the circles (**a–e**) shown below. Give your answers to two decimal places.

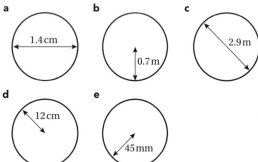

a 1.4 cm **b** 0.7 m **c** 2.9 m

d 12 cm **e** 45 mm

2 Work out the area of each of the following shapes (**a–g**). Give your answers to three significant figures.

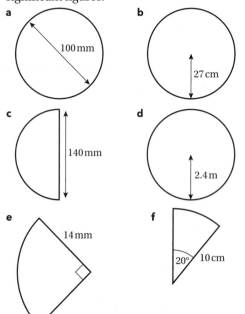

a 100 mm **b** 27 cm

c 140 mm **d** 2.4 m

e 14 mm **f** 20° 10 cm

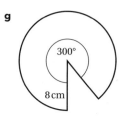

g 300° 8 cm

3 A mobile phone mast provides a clear signal for up to 6.5 km in all directions. Calculate the area that has good signal.

4 A staffroom contains a rectangular table 1.3 m by 0.8 m and a circular table of radius 0.55 m. Which table top has the larger work area?

5 A round table with a diameter of 1.2 m is covered with a circular table cloth that extends 15 cm below the level of the table (all around it). What is the area of the table cloth?

6 A circle has an area of 6 cm². What is its radius?

7 A rotating water spray covers an area of 7 m². How far away from the sprayer would you need to stand to make sure you were outside the watering area?

8 A park contains two flower beds, each with an area of 31.5 m². One is circular, the other is square. Which one has the greater perimeter? Show how you worked this out.

Section 3: Area of composite shapes
HOMEWORK 11D

1 Calculate the area of each of the following shapes (**a–f**).

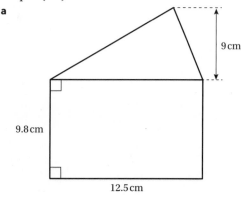

a 9 cm 9.8 cm 12.5 cm

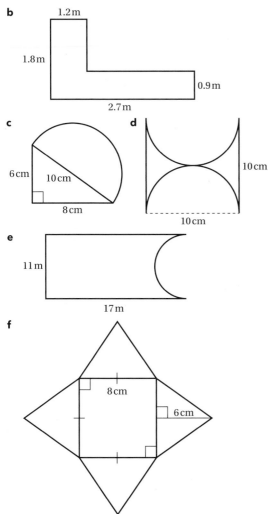

b
1.2 m
1.8 m
0.9 m
2.7 m

c
6 cm
10 cm
8 cm

d
10 cm
10 cm

e
11 m
17 m

f
8 cm
6 cm

e
9
13
14
14
15

f
1
3 6
3
6
2

g
14

h
20
25 30
30
40
95

i
45
90 90

2 Work out the area of the shaded section of each of the following shapes (**a**–**i**). Show your working clearly. All dimensions are in centimetres.

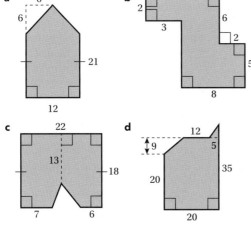

a
6
6
21
12

b
2
3
6
2
5
8

c
22
13
18
7 6

d
12
9
5
20 35
20

3 Find the area of the shapes (**a**–**f**) shown below. Give your answers to three significant figures.

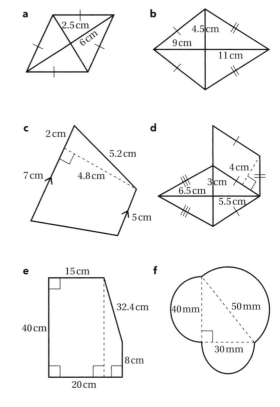

a
2.5 cm
6 cm

b
4.5 cm
9 cm
11 cm

c
2 cm
5.2 cm
7 cm
4.8 cm
5 cm

d
4 cm
6.5 cm
3 cm
5.5 cm

e
15 cm
32.4 cm
40 cm
8 cm
20 cm

f
40 mm
50 mm
30 mm

31

4 The shapes (**a–f**) below are all made up of circles and squares or parts thereof. Calculate the area of each shaded part giving your answers to two decimal places. The dimensions are all in centimetres.

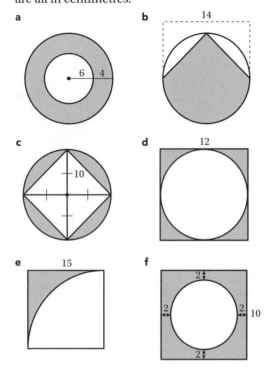

a

b 14

c 10

d 12

e 15

f 2 2 2 10 2

HOMEWORK 11E

1 A 1.2 m wide path is built around a circular pond of diameter 3.8 m.
  a Work out the area of the surface of the pond.
  b Work out the area of the path.
  c What is the combined area of the surface of the pond and the path?

2 A DVD has a diameter of 12 cm. There is a round hole in the centre of the disk and it has a diameter of 15 mm.
  a The top surface of the disk is to be printed with a logo. What is the total area available for printing?
  b The disks are packed in rectangular boxes 130 mm × 190 mm. Work out the area of plastic visible when the disk is in place on the base of the box as shown shaded in the diagram.
  c What is the total perimeter of the disk?

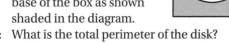

GCSE
MATHS

3 The designs (**a–c**) below are printed on square disks with an area of 30 cm². Which of the designs requires the most black paint?

a b c

4 A round rug of diameter 2.4 m is placed on the floor of a rectangular room 3.2 m × 4.1 m. How much floor space is clear once the rug is in place?

5 A large circular pizza has a diameter of 25 cm. If it is cut into 8 equal slices, what is the area of each slice?

6 The small indoor pool at a community centre is rectangular with a semicircular shallow area at one end. The rectangular part of the pool is 10 m long and 4.3 m wide. There is a 2 m wide non-slip area around the pool, as shown in the diagram below.

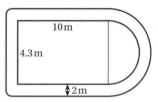

10 m
4.3 m
2 m

  a What is the area of the non-slip flooring?
  b Half the flooring has to be resurfaced at a cost of £132.50 per square metre. What will this cost?
  c The bottom of the pool is to be painted with an antifungal paint. Work out the total floor area to be painted.
  d The paint comes in 2 litre tins, each with a coverage area of 20 000 cm². How many tins will be needed to paint the floor of the pool?

Chapter 11 review

Give all your answers to three significant figures where appropriate.

1 A circular plate on a cooker has a diameter of 21 cm. There is a metal strip around the outside of the plate.
  a Work out the area of the cooking surface of the plate.

b What is the length of the metal strip?

c Will a round frying pan with a base of area 397 cm² fit onto this cooking plate with no overlap? Show how you decided this.

2 What is the radius of a circle with an area of 65 cm²?

3 Calculate the shaded area of each of the shapes (**a**–**g**) shown below.

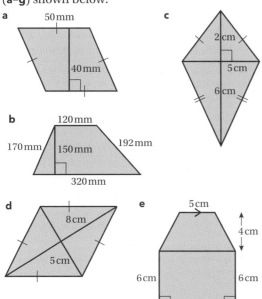

a 50 mm, 40 mm

b 120 mm, 170 mm, 150 mm, 192 mm, 320 mm

c 2 cm, 5 cm, 6 cm

d 8 cm, 5 cm

e 5 cm, 4 cm, 6 cm, 6 cm, 12 cm

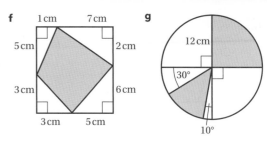

f 1 cm, 7 cm, 5 cm, 2 cm, 3 cm, 6 cm, 3 cm, 5 cm

g 12 cm, 30°, 10°

4 Shape MNOP, shown below, is a trapezium with an area of 150 m². Calculate the length of NO.

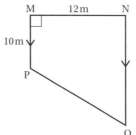

M — 12 m — N, 10 m, P, O

5 The search area for a missing hiker has been narrowed down to the shaded area of this sector of a national park as shown in the diagram below. Work out the area of the park that needs to be searched.

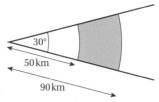

30°, 50 km, 90 km

12 Rounding and estimation

Section 1: Approximate values
HOMEWORK 12A

1 Round these numbers to the nearest 100.
   a 2345   **b** 27 907   **c** 143

2 Round these measurements to the nearest whole unit.
   a 8.6 cm   **b** 13.14 m   **c** 0.1987 m

3 Round each value to the nearest million.
   a 13 499 000   **b** 1 987 654   **c** 21 097 099

4 Say whether each value will round to £10 or not.
   a £9.56   **b** £10.56   **c** £10.45   **d** £10.09

HOMEWORK 12B

1 Write the following fractions as decimals to two decimal places.
   a $\frac{1}{9}$ **b** $\frac{2}{3}$ **c** $\frac{5}{9}$ **d** $\frac{3}{11}$

2 Write the following values to one decimal place.
   a 4.197   **b** 30.048   **c** 6.329   **d** 6.392

3 Round each amount of money in the lists to the nearest pound. Write an estimated total amount for each list.

List A	List B	List C	List D
3.89	3.49	3.69	203.19
0.19	1.19	17.99	199.99
1.99	0.39	1.69	201.09
2.10	2.29	0.75	107.25
3.89	11.99	14.29	124.50
		0.99	89.04
		12.29	

4 Using the information from question 3, calculate the difference between your estimated total for each list and the actual total amount.

5 For each of the following situations, round the given values to a suitable level of accuracy.
  a Amit runs 100 m in 13 seconds. He covers about 7.692307 m in a second.
  b £7.45 is shared equally among 8 people. Each person should get £0.93125
  c A plane travels 4200 km in 7.75 hours. This is a speed of 541.9354839 km/h.
  d Apply fertiliser at a rate of 0.3947 l/m².

HOMEWORK 12C

1 How many significant figures are there in each of these values?
  a 345   **b** 12.096
  c 0.00188   **d** 8.0
  e 0.007   **f** 0.120

2 Round each of these numbers to three significant figures.
  a 53 217   **b** 712984
  c 17.364   **d** 0.007279

3 Round 24.738095 to:
  a two significant figures
  b five significant figures.

4 Round 0.0024835 to:
  a four significant figures
  b one significant figure.

HOMEWORK 12D

1 For each of the values (**i**–**x**) below complete the actions (**a**–**d**).
  i 98.847   **ii** 5.4396
  iii 239.364   **iv** 0.009786
  v 2017.968   **vi** 4.6984
  vii 0.008898   **viii** 125.7449
  ix 5023.505   **x** 0.7654
  a Round values to two decimal places.
  b Truncate values to two decimal places.
  c Truncate values to a whole number.
  d Truncate after the third significant figure.

2 A computer criminal was caught stealing money from bank clients. He had adapted a computer program to truncate the interest amounts due on accounts after four decimal places. So, an interest amount of £100.089775 would transfer to the account as £100.0897 and the 0.000075 would be paid to the criminal's account. He had being doing this for 15 years before he was caught.
  a Why do you think this went unnoticed for so long?
  b How many transactions would need to be processed for the criminal to earn a pound?

Section 2: Approximation and estimation

HOMEWORK 12E

1 Use whole numbers to show why:
  a $3.9 \times 5.1 \approx 20$ **b** $68 \times 5.03 \approx 350$
  c $999 \times 6.9 \approx 7000$ **d** $42.02 \div 5.96 \approx 7$

2 Josh is paid £8.45 per hour. He normally works 38 hours per week.
  a Estimate his weekly earnings to the nearest pound.
  b Estimate approximately how much he earns in a year if he takes two weeks off for holidays.

3 Give an estimated answer for each calculation.
  a 0.82×21.75 **b** 0.816×0.207
  c 140.7×5.9 **d** 12.35×0.025
  e 12.45×8.89 **f** $(4.25 \times 12.15) \div 7.3$

4 Estimate the answers to each of these calculations to the nearest whole number.
  a 9.75×4.108
  b $0.0387 \div 0.00732$
  c $\dfrac{39.4 \times 6.32}{9.987}$
  d $\sqrt{64.25} \times (3.098)^2$

5 Estimate the answer to each calculation to the nearest whole number.
  a $5.2 + 16.9 - 8.9 + 7.1$
  b $(23.86 + 9.07) \div (15.99 - 4.59)$
  c $9.3 \times \dfrac{7.6}{5.9} \times 0.95$
  d $(8.9)^2 \times \sqrt{8.98}$

6 Write down an approximate calculation to show that $5.78 \times £51.30$ is about £300.

7 A fast-food outlet uses a ticket system to serve people. In one hour, they served 394 customers. Each customer spent an average of £3.09. Estimate the total earnings per hour for this store.

8 **a** Find an approximate answer to $(3.802 + 7.54) \div 3.27$
  b Calculate the value of $(3.802 + 7.54) \div 3.27$ and then give your answer to two significant figures.

Section 3: Limits of accuracy
HOMEWORK 12F

1 Each of the numbers below have been rounded to the degree of accuracy shown in the brackets. Write down the error interval for each number using inequality notation and the variable letter shown.
  a 42 (nearest whole number) x
  b 400 (1 sf) x
  c 12.24 (2 dp) x
  d 2.5 (to nearest tenth) x
  e 390 (nearest ten) x
  f 60 cm (nearest 10 cm) L
  g 5.6 cm (nearest mm) L
  h 28 g (nearest gram) w
  i 6.5 seconds (nearest $\frac{1}{10}$th of a second) t
  j 1.23 litres (3 sf) v

2 A building is 72 m tall measured to the nearest metre.
  a What is the least and greatest height the building could be?
  b Is 72.499999999999999999 metres a possible height for the building? Give a reason why or why not.

3 Jess took 25.7 seconds to complete a maths problem. The time was measured to the nearest tenth of a second. Between which values could the actual time lie? Give your answer as an inequality using t for time.

Chapter 12 review

1 Round each of the following numbers to the accuracy shown in brackets
  a 15.638 (1 dp)   **b** 383 452 345 (3 sf)
  c 0.000034556 (2 sf)   **d** 0.99998 (3 dp)

2 Estimate the value of each of the following.
  a $\sqrt{6.1} + 2.9$ **b** 14.6×2.7
  c $46.2 \div 25.3$ **d** $(23.4)^2$
  e 125×384 **f** $\dfrac{36.5 + 28.2}{29.9 + 4.8}$
  g $\sqrt{49.1 \times 24.8}$ **h** $\dfrac{\sqrt{99.6}}{\sqrt{143}}$

3 Tayo's height is 1.62 m, to the nearest centimetre. Calculate the least possible and greatest possible height that he could be.

4 A child is weighed at a clinic and her mass is recorded to the nearest half kilogram as 12.5 kg. What is the greatest and least possible mass of this child?

13 Percentages

Section 1: Review of percentages
HOMEWORK 13A

1. Write the following fractions and decimals as percentages.
   a 0.75   b 0.6   c 0.08   d 0.632
   e $\frac{1}{2}$ f $\frac{4}{5}$ g $\frac{7}{8}$ h $\frac{1}{20}$

   Tip

   'Percent' means 'out of a hundred'.

2. Write each of following percentages as a common fraction in its simplest terms.
   a 45%   b 90%   c 70%   d 37.5%
   e 40%   f 88%   g 65%   h 32%

3. Write the decimal equivalent of each percentage.
   a 78%   b 99%   c 35%
   d 48%   e 0.6%   f 0.09%

4. a If 94.5% of houses in the UK have a TV set, what percentage do not?
   b If $\frac{3}{4}$ of mobile phones are sold as pay-as-you-go, what percentage are not?
   c 0.245 of computer users back up their work every day. What percentage do not do this?

5. Bjorn spends 31.7% of a day asleep, 0.127 of the day doing house work and $\frac{4}{9}$ of the day at work. What percentage of the day is spent doing other things?

6. Anya pays 0.12 of her salary into her savings account. What percentage of her salary is this?

7. Barry gets the following marks for three tests: $\frac{31}{50}, \frac{17}{35}, \frac{51}{80}$
   a In which test did he get the best marks?
   b What is his mean result for the three tests as a percentage to the nearest whole number?

Section 2: Percentage calculations
HOMEWORK 13B

You are allowed to use a calculator for these questions.

1. Calculate:
   a 5% of 150   b 8% of 300
   c 30% of 150   d 22% of 50
   e 120% of 70   f 150% of 80

   Tip

   To find a percentage of a quantity, multiply by the percentage and divide the result by 100.

2. Calculate the following giving your answers as mixed numbers or decimals as necessary.
   a 17% of £400   b 70% of 65 kg
   c 3.5% of 80 minutes   d 6.3% of £1000
   e 4.7% of 210 m

3. Annie got 65% for a test that was out of 60 marks.
   a How many marks did she get in this test?
   b She gets the same percentage score in a test that is out of 80. How many marks did she get in this test?

4. A machine in a factory has a failure rate of 2.5%. If the machine makes 15 200 items per day, how many are defective?

5. Approximately 72% of homes put the correct recycling bin out every week, the rest do not. In a city of 32 904, how many homes:
   a put out the correct bin?
   b don't put out the correct bin?

6. A laptop is advertised for sale for £549 excluding VAT. VAT is charged at 20%.
   a How much extra is the VAT?
   b How much is the total cost of the laptop?

7 9.5% of a 864 hectare farm grows wheat and the rest is used to grow barley. How many hectares of land is used to grow:

a wheat?

b barley?

8 The cost of energy used in Banjul's house increases by 63% in the three months of winter compared to the three months of summer. If the cost in the summer is £205:

a what is the increase in cost in the winter?

b how much is the fuel bill for the winter?

HOMEWORK 13C

1 Express the first amount as a percentage of the second. Give your answer to no more than two decimal places (if necessary).

a 200 m of 4 km

b 32 m of 4 km

c 125 m of 2 km

d 12 cm of 3 m

e 15 mm of 6 cm

f 23 cm of 5 m

g 45 pence of £6

h 62 pence of £4.50

i 12 seconds of a minute

Tip

To find one quantity as the percentage of another, divide the first quantity by the second quantity and multiply the result by 100.

2 Sanjita got 21 out of 26 for an assignment and Niall got 23 out of 30. Who got the highest percentage mark? What was this mark?

3 In a school election there were 1248 students eligible to vote. Of these, 1008 voted. What was the percentage voter turnout?

4 Mel improved his swimming time for the 200 m backstroke race by 3 seconds. If his previous best time was 2 minutes and 20 seconds, what is his percentage improvement? Give your answer to one decimal place.

Section 3: Percentage change
HOMEWORK 13D

1 Increase each amount by the percentage given.

a £36 by 20% b £600 by 45%

c £40 by 6.5% d £4500 by 12%

e £625 by 4% f £456 by 4.6%

Tip

The quick way to find a percentage increase or decrease is to find the multiplier.

2 Decrease each amount by the percentage given.

a £54 by 10% b £560 by 24%

c £862 by 14.5% d £632 by 7.4%

e £278 by 5.3% f £34 900 by 15.7%

3 House prices in a city have increased by 3.1% in a year. How much would a house be worth at the end of the year if it was priced at £345 000 at the start of the year?

4 Sammy has been offered a pay rise of £20 per week or a 5% increase on his hourly rate. If he earns £7.40 per hour for a 37.5 hour week, would he be better taking the £20 or the percentage increase? If he chooses the better option, how much would he earn in a week?

5 The cost of being a member of a golf club has decreased by 15% in a year. If last year's cost was £485, what is the cost this year to the nearest £?

6 Shares in a building company were worth £12.15 each to start with. After six months their value had decreased by 20%.

a Find the value of one share after 6 months.

b Six months later their value had risen again by 20%. Are the shares worth the same amount as they were originally? Give a reason for your answer.

HOMEWORK 13E

1 Find the original values if:

a 20% is £8 b 6% is 39.6 kg

c 140% is 840 g d 105% is £472.50

2 New cars depreciate in value (their value decreases) significantly in their first year. Copy and complete the table to show the value of these cars at the end of their first year.

Car	Original price	Depreciation	New value
A	£26 200	32%	
B	£16 800	17%	
C	£36 500	26%	

3 In a small village school nine pupils are in Year 6. This is 15% of the school population.
  a How many pupils are there in the school?
  b How many pupils are not in Year 6?

4 Mick has had a 7.4% pay rise. If his new salary is £36 730.80, what was his salary before the rise?

5 Keith is training for a triathlon. His overall time has improved by 3% since he began his training. His new personal best is now 5 hours and 24 minutes. What was his old personal best (to the nearest minute)?

Chapter 13 review

1 Write the following percentages as fractions in their simplest form.
  a 35% **b** 20% **c** 2.5%

2 Express each of these fractions or decimals as a percentage.
  a $\frac{4}{5}$ **b** $\frac{1}{3}$
  c $\frac{7}{16}$ **d** 0.6
  e 0.07 **f** 0.003

3 The value of a vintage car increased from £140 000 to £151 200.
  What percentage increase is this?

4 The value of a car was £45 600 when it was new. After 2 years it had lost 54.5% of its value. How much was it worth after two years?

5 Vlad has a machine that makes golf tees at 45 per minute. He wants to increase the speed of the machine by 9%. How many whole tees will the machine make per minute if he is successful?

6 Express:
  a 45 pence as a percentage of £3
  b 240 g as a percentage of 4 kg.

7 The table below shows the nine most popular marathon races in 2013.

Marathon	Number of starters	Number of finishers
New York	47 000	46 759
Chicago	45 000	37 455
Berlin	40 987	34 377
Paris	40 000	32 980
London	37 000	36 672
Tokyo	36 000	34 678
Osaka	30 000	27 157
Honolulu	30 000	23 786
Marine Corps (Washington D.C.)	30 000	23 515

  a Which of these races can claim to have the best finishing percentage?
  b Express the number of starters in London as a percentage of the number of starters in New York.
  c Can you use the data to decide which marathon is the toughest? Give a reason for your answer.

8 The average (mean) house price in the UK (according to the Office of National Statistics) at the end of 2013 was £250 000.
  a If house prices rose by 8% on average in 2014, what would be the average house price at the end of 2014?
  b House prices increased by 5.5% in 2013. What was the average price at the end of 2012?

14 Powers and roots

Section 1: Index notation
HOMEWORK 14A

1 Write each of the following in index notation. You can leave the answer in index form.

a $3 \times 3 \times 3$

b $8 \times 8 \times 8 \times 8 \times 8 \times 8$

c $9 \times 9 \times 9 \times 9 \times 9 \times 9 \times 9 \times 9$

d $11 \times 11 \times 11 \times 11$

e 8 to the power of 7

f 7 to the power of 8

g 6 multiplied by itself 9 times

h 7 multiplied by itself 7 times

i 9 multiplied by itself

j $a \times a \times a \times a$

k $m \times m \times m \times m \times m \times m \times m \times m \times m$

l n multiplied by itself 5 times.

> **Tip**
>
> $4 \times 4 \times 4 = 4^3$ in index notation

2 Convert these numbers to their expanded form. You do not need to work out the answer.

a 4^3 b 7^4 c 16^4 d 21^8

e 154^6 f 143^5 g 2.5^6

3 Evaluate each expression without using a calculator.

a 3^3 b 8^2 c 5^3

d $3^2 + 2^3$ e $4^3 + 2^2$ f $5^2 - 2^2$

g $4^2 \times 5^2$ h $2^5 \div 2^1$ i $3^5 \div 3^2$

HOMEWORK 14B

1 Use your calculator to evaluate the following.

a 5^6 b 13^4 c 12^3

d 10^5 e 24^2 f 20^3

> **Tip**
>
> Remember that the order of operations says you must calculate the powers first.

2 Use a calculator to find the value of each expression.

a $13^3 - 3^5$ b $14^3 \times 13^2$ c $3^7 + 3^5$

d $6^6 + 2^5$ e $24^3 \div 6^3$

3 Copy each question part and fill in $<$ or $>$ to make each statement true.

a $5^6 \square 6^5$ b $10^4 \square 4^{10}$ c $11^2 \square 2^{11}$

d $11^{10} \square 10^{11}$ e $5^{10} \square 10^5$

HOMEWORK 14C

1 Write each of the following using positive indices only.

a 3^{-1} b 6^{-1} c 7^{-1}

d 5^{-2} e 2^{-3} f 2^{-5}

g 3^{-5} h 7^{-6} i 24^{-3}

> **Tip**
>
> Remember $4^{-1} = \dfrac{1}{4}$

2 Express the following with negative indices.

a $\dfrac{1}{4}$ b $\dfrac{1}{8}$ c $\dfrac{1}{2^2}$ d $\dfrac{1}{4^3}$

e $\dfrac{1}{2^4}$ f $\dfrac{1}{9^5}$ g $\dfrac{1}{7^3}$ h $\dfrac{1}{11^4}$

3 Copy each question part and fill in $=$ or $\neq$ to make each statement true.

> **Tip**
>
> Remember $\neq$ means 'not equal to'.

a $10^{-2} \square \dfrac{1}{10^2}$ b $7^0 \square 1$

c $10^{-2} \square \dfrac{2}{10}$ d $6^{-3} \square \dfrac{1}{6^3}$

e $8^{-3} \square \dfrac{3}{8}$ f $\dfrac{1}{11^5} \square 11^{-5}$

Section 2: The laws of indices
HOMEWORK 14D

1. Simplify. Leave the answers in index notation.
   a $2^3 \times 2^5$ **b** $10^6 \times 10^3$ **c** $3^4 \times 3^6$
   d $4^3 \times 4^{-5}$ **e** $2^{-3} \times 2^7$ **f** $3^0 \times 3^4$
   g $3 \times 3^2 \times 3^{-6}$ **h** $4^3 \times 4^2 \times 4$ **i** $10^4 \times 10^{-6} \times 10^2$

> **Tip**
>
> Learn the laws of indices.

2. Simplify. Leave the answers in index notation.
   a $7^4 \div 7^2$ **b** $10^5 \div 10^3$ **c** $10^6 \div 10^2$
   d $4^{10} \div 4^0$ **e** $5^6 \div 5$ **f** $10^6 \div 10^6$
   g $\dfrac{5^3}{5^{-3}}$ **h** $\dfrac{10^7}{10^{-3}}$ **i** $\dfrac{3^{-4}}{3^{-5}}$ **j** $\dfrac{3^0}{3^4}$

3. Simplify each expression. Give the answers in index notation.
   a $(4^3)^3$ **b** $(3^2)^3$ **c** $(5^5)^2$ **d** $(9^3)^2$
   e $(5^4)^{-3}$ **f** $(8^{-2})^2$ **g** $(10^2)^{-3}$ **h** $(7^5)^{-2}$
   i $(8^4)^0$ **j** $(3^3 \times 3^4)^2$

4. Say whether each statement is true or false. If it is false, write the correct answer.
   a $4^2 \times 4^5 = 4^7$ **b** $5^6 \div 5^2 = 5^3$ **c** $10^9 \div 10^3 = 10^6$
   d $(7^3)^2 = 7^5$ **e** $19^0 = 1$ **f** $(5^2)^0 = 5$

Section 3: Working with powers and roots
HOMEWORK 14E

1. Draw up a table like Table A at the bottom of the page.
   a Use a calculator to work out the missing values in the table. Some powers of 5 have been done as an example.
   b Compare the positive and negative values for the same index. What do you notice?

Table A

Index Base	−3	−2	−1	0	1	2	3	4
5	$5^{-3} = \frac{1}{125}$	$5^{-2} =$	$5^{-1} = \frac{1}{5}$	$5^0 = 1$	$5^1 = 5$	$5^2 = 25$	$5^3 =$	$5^4 =$
6								
7								
8								
9								
10								

2. **a** Copy and complete Table B (below). Any number can be written as a sum of powers of 2.
   For example, $29 = 2^4 + 2^3 + 2^2 + 2^0$
   b Work out the numbers given by these sums of powers of 2.
      i $2^8 + 2^4 + 2^3$
      ii $2^{10} + 2^7 + 2^0$
      iii $2^6 + 2^3 + 2^1 + 2^0$
   c Write the numbers from 1 to 30 as sums of powers of 2.
   d Write these numbers as sums of powers of 2.
      i 52   **ii** 91   **iii** 143

Table B

Index Base	0	1	2	3	4	5
2	$2^0 = 1$	$2^1 = 2$	$2^2 = 4$	$2^3 =$	$2^4 =$	$2^5 =$

Index Base	6	7	8	9	10
2	$2^6 =$	$2^7 =$	$2^8 =$	$2^9 =$	$2^{10} =$

HOMEWORK 14F

1. Decide whether each statement is true or false.
   a $3^6 = 6^3$ **b** $3^5 > 4^5$ **c** $5^0 = 3^0$
   d $3^1 = 3^{-1}$ **e** $3^4 > 4^3$ **f** $6^7 < 7^6$
   g $6^2 = 2^6$ **h** $9^5 > 5^9$ **i** $4^{-3} > 3^{-4}$
   j $4^{-3} = \dfrac{1}{2}$ **k** $7^{-1} = 8^{-1}$ **l** $3(3^{-1}) = 1$

2. Use your table from Exercise 14E of the Student Book to work these out without using a calculator.
   a $\sqrt{25}$ **b** $\sqrt[3]{8}$ **c** $\sqrt[4]{256}$
   d $\sqrt[3]{125}$ **e** $\sqrt[5]{243}$ **f** $\sqrt[3]{64}$
   g $\sqrt[3]{8} + \sqrt[4]{625}$ **h** $\sqrt{2500}$ **i** $\sqrt[5]{32} + \sqrt[4]{81}$
   j $\sqrt[3]{27\,000}$ **k** $\sqrt[4]{160\,000}$ **l** $\sqrt[5]{3125} \times \sqrt[4]{625}$

HOMEWORK 14G

1. Find the lengths of the sides of each of the three square areas (**a**–**c**) shown below.

   a Area = 25 cm² **b** Area = 0.36 m² **c** Area = 900 mm²

2. Julia has 6400 square mosaic tiles. Is it possible to arrange them to make a square?

3. Shandy has a square piece of plastic with sides of 120 cm. Is this big enough to cover a square table with an area of 1.4 m²?

4. Malcolm wants to tile a square area in his bathroom of length 4.3 m. The square tiles he plans to use each have an area of 784 cm².
   a How large is the area he wishes to tile?
   b What is the length of one side of each tile?
   c How many tiles will he need to tile his area? Show your working.
   d He knows from experience that he needs to buy 15% more than he needs in case of breakages. How many boxes of tiles should he buy if they come nine to a box?
   e The tiles cost £24.50 per box. How much will it cost him to buy the tiles he needs (including the 15% extra)?

5. In a pizza restaurant, children's pizzas are half the price of full-size pizzas, as the diameter is 15 cm compared to 30 cm.
   a Use the formula
   $$\text{area} = 3.14 \times \left(\frac{1}{2} \times \text{diameter}\right)^2$$ to work out the area of each pizza to two decimal places.
   b What would be the best buy if you took two children for a pizza?

6. Work out the length of the sides of each of the cubes (**a**–**c**) in the diagram below.

   a Volume = 125 cm³ **b** Volume = 729 cm³ **c** Volume = 3.375 m³

Tip

Volume of a cube = $L \times L \times L$

7. Sam received an inheritance of £3500. She wants to invest it for ten years in an account that offers 4% growth but she wants to know how much money she will have at the end of the ten-year period. The bank tells Sam that the formula they use is as follows.
   value of future investment
   = original amount $\times (1.04)^{10}$
   a Work out how much money Sam will have in the account at the end of ten years.
   b How much will she have if she decides to spend £1000 and put the rest of the money into this account?

8. Pierre took a mortgage of £75 000 to buy a flat. The bank manager showed him this formula for working out how much he will repay over a 25-year period.
   total amount paid
   = mortgage amount $\times (1.05)^{25}$
   a Work out how much his mortgage will cost if Pierre takes 25 years to repay it.
   b The power of 25 in the formula represents the number of years over which it is repaid. Work out what the total amount paid would be if Pierre paid his mortgage off in 20 years.
   c How much would he save by paying over the shorter period?

Chapter 14 review

1. Write each number in index form.
   a $6 \times 6 \times 6 \times 6 \times 6$
   b Five cubed
   c Eight squared
   d Seventeen to the power of six

2. Write each expression in expanded form and work out the answer.
   a 3^4 **b** 6^3 **c** $(5^6 \div 5^5) \times 11^2$

3. Put these expressions in order from smallest to largest.
   a $4^4, \sqrt{64}, 12^2, 3^3, 5 \times \sqrt{144}$
   b $6^5, 5^6, 10^4, 92^0, 5^2, 15^2$

4 Write these numbers with positive indices.
  a 6^{-4} **b** 4^{-11} **c** 7^{-3}

5 Use the laws of indices to simplify each expression and write it as a single power of 6.
  a $6^3 \times 6^2$ **b** $6^5 \times 6^{-3}$ **c** $6^8 \div 6^3$
  d $6^3 \div 6^6$ **e** $(6^2)^3$ **f** $(6^{-3})^3$

6 Evaluate. Check your answers with a calculator.
  a $\sqrt{169}$ **b** $\sqrt{0.16}$ **c** $\sqrt[3]{64}$
  d $\sqrt[4]{16}$ **e** $\sqrt[4]{625}$ **f** $\sqrt{\dfrac{1}{16}}$

7 Find the length of each side of a cube of volume 0.008 m^3.

8 $\dfrac{V}{20} = \sqrt{h}$. Find V when $h = 16$.

9 $P - y = x^2$. Find P when $x = 3$ and $y = 9$.

10 Electricians use the formula $V = \sqrt{PR}$ to work out voltage (V) when P is the power in watts and R is the resistance in ohms. Calculate the voltage when $P = 2500$ watts and $R = 21.16$ ohms.

15 Standard form

Section 1: Expressing numbers in standard form
HOMEWORK 15A

1 Express each of the following in standard form.
  a 425 000 **b** 45 000
  c 5 020 000 **d** 0.06
  e 0.0002 **f** 511 000
  g 0.000001542 **h** 0.00000002652
  i 0.058

> **Tip**
>
> The index number tells you how far and in which direction the number needs adjusting.

2 Express each of the following real-life quantities in standard form.
  a In 2014 the population of China was estimated to be 1 366 000 000.
  b The distance from the Earth to the Sun is approximately 149 600 000 km.
  c The Earth is thought to be 4 600 000 000 years old.
  d A hydrogen atom has a radius of 0.00000000001 m.
  e The density of the core of the Sun is 150 000 kg/m^3
  f The wavelength of violet light is 0.0000004 m.

HOMEWORK 15B

1 Express each of the following as an ordinary number.
  a 3.6×10^3 **b** 6.2×10^5
  c 7.9×10^2 **d** 6.215×10^5
  e 3.05×10^{-4} **f** 1.28×10^{-5}
  g 5×10^{-8}

2 Write each quantity out in full as an ordinary number.
  a The Earth orbits the Sun at 2.98×10^4 metres per second.
  b The Moon is 3.84×10^8 km away from the Earth.
  c The Sun is 1.5×10^{11} metres away from the Earth on average.
  d There are thought to be 8×10^{10} stars in the Milky Way galaxy.
  e The smallest observable and measurable object is currently 1×10^{-18} m.
  f The mass of an atom of plutonium–239 is 6.645×10^{-27} g.

Section 2: Calculators and standard form
HOMEWORK 15C

1 Enter each of these numbers into your calculator using the correct function key and write down what appears on the display.

a 6.3×10^{11} **b** 1.9×10^{-6}

c 5.7×10^{7} **d** 1.94×10^{-3}

e 1.52×10^{-10} **f** 4.86×10^{6}

g 3.309×10^{-7} **h** 3.081×10^{6}

Tip

Make sure you fully understand how your calculator represents standard form.

2 There are six different calculator displays in the diagrams below giving answers in exponential form. Write each answer (**a–f**) correctly in standard form.

a `7.8ε16`
b `4.8ε+16`
c `6.-8`

d `1.5ε-5`
e `2.5ε-20`
f `2.3+8`

HOMEWORK 15D

1 Use your calculator to do these calculations. Give your answers in standard form to three significant figures.

a 4582^7 **b** $(0.00003)^5$

c $0.0008 \div 1200^5$ **d** $76\,000\,000 \div 0.000007$

e $(0.0036)^4 \times (0.00275)^7$ **f** $(56 \times 274)^3$

g $4489 \times \dfrac{8630}{0.00006}$ **h** $\dfrac{7300}{0.0002^5}$

i $\sqrt{7.49} \times 10^6$ **j** $\sqrt[3]{8.1 \times 10^{-11}}$

Section 3: Working in standard form

HOMEWORK 15E

1 Simplify, giving the answers in standard form.

a $(3 \times 10^{11}) \times (5 \times 10^{12})$

b $(6.4 \times 10^{9}) \times (2 \times 10^{5})$

c $(9 \times 10^{15}) \div (3 \times 10^{10})$

d $(2.6 \times 10^{7}) \div (7 \times 10^{3})$

e $(5.8 \times 10^{54}) \div (6 \times 10^{25})$

2 Simplify each of the following giving all answers in standard form.

a $(3 \times 10^{-3}) \times (6 \times 10^{-17})$

b $(1.3 \times 10^{-9}) \times (6 \times 10^{-5})$

c $(1.8 \times 10^{-7}) \times (7.1 \times 10^{-2})$

d $(12 \times 10^{-6}) \times (5 \times 10^{3})$

e $(8 \times 10^{16}) \div (9.2 \times 10^{-13})$

f $(8 \times 10^{-22}) \div (1 \times 10^{17})$

3 Carry out these calculations without using your calculator. Leave the answer in standard form.

a $(4 \times 10^{13}) \times (5 \times 10^{15})$

b $(5.5 \times 10^{7}) \times (6 \times 10^{4})$

c $(6 \times 10^{10})^3$

d $(1.7 \times 10^{-5}) \times (1.8 \times 10^{-7})$

e $(0.6 \times 10^{16}) \times (0.3 \times 10^{11})$

f $(7 \times 10^{15}) \div (8 \times 10^{13})$

g $(1.68 \times 10^{9}) \div (8 \times 10^{6})$

h $(7 \times 10^{-10}) \div (8 \times 10^{-14})$

4 The speed of light is approximately 3×10^8 metres per second. How far will the light travel in:

a 15 seconds?   **b** 30 seconds?

c 10^3 seconds?   **d** 3×10^5 seconds?

5 There are approximately 1.1×10^{14} cells in each human body.

a How many cells would there be in a class of 30 students? Give the answer in standard form and as an ordinary number.

b If there were 7.2×10^9 people on Earth, how many human cells are there on the planet?

HOMEWORK 15F

1 Carry out these calculations without using a calculator. Give your answers in standard form.

a $(4 \times 10^{7}) + (2 \times 10^{7})$

b $(4 \times 10^{-4}) - (1.5 \times 10^{-4})$

c $(2.5 \times 10^{6}) + (3 \times 10^{7})$

d $(7 \times 10^{8}) - (4 \times 10^{7})$

e $(6 \times 10^{-5}) + (3 \times 10^{-4})$

f $(8 \times 10^{-3}) - (2.5 \times 10^{-5})$

2 Mars has a surface area of approximately $1.45 \times 10^8 \, \text{km}^2$ and the Earth has a surface area of approximately $5.1 \times 10^8 \, \text{km}^2$.

a Which planet has the greater surface area?

b What is the difference between the surface areas of the two planets?

c Saturn has a surface area of $4.27 \times 10^{10} \, \text{km}^2$. What is the difference between the surface area of Saturn and:

     i Mars?   **ii** Earth?

3 The Earth is approximately 1.5×10^8 km from the Sun and Mercury is approximately 5.79×10^7 km from the Sun.

a What is the closest distance possible between the two planets?

b What is the maximum possible distance between the two planets?

Chapter 15 review

1 Use a calculator and give the answers in standard form.

   a $5 \times 10^4 + 9 \times 10^6$

   b $3.27 \times 10^{-3} \times 2.4 \times 10^2$

   c $5(8.1 \times 10^9 - 2 \times 10^7)$

   d $(3.2 \times 10^{-1}) - (2.33 \times 10^{-3})$ (to 3 sf)

2 Simplify the following without using a calculator and give the answers in standard form.

   a $(5.26 \times 10^7) + (8.2 \times 10^7)$

   b $(8.2 \times 10^5) \times (6.3 \times 10^9)$

   c $(6 \times 10^4) + (5 \times 10^3)$

   d $(3 \times 10^6) \div (2 \times 10^5)$

3 The UK has an approximate area of $2.4 \times 10^5 \, \text{km}^2$. The USA has an area of approximately $9.8 \times 10^6 \, \text{km}^2$.

   a What is the difference in the areas of the two countries? Give the answer in standard form.

   b What is the combined area of the two countries? Give the answer in standard form.

   c How many times bigger is the area of the USA than the area of the UK?

16 Further algebra

Section 1: Multiplying two binomials

HOMEWORK 16A

1 Expand and collect like terms.

   a $(x + 1)(x + 4)$ **b** $(x + 3)(x + 5)$

   c $(a + 5)(a + 4)$ **d** $(6 + x)(3 + x)$

   e $(7 + x)(x + 2)$ **f** $(a + 6)(7 + a)$

> **Tip**
>
> Each term in a bracket must be multiplied by each term in the other bracket.

2 Find these products and simplify.

   a $(x - 4)(x - 2)$

   b $(a - 6)(a - 3)$

   c $(m + 3)(m - 6)$

   d $(p - 7)(p + 5)$

   e $(x - 8)(x + 5)$

   f $(x + 12)(x - 2)$

3 Expand and simplify.

   a $(2x + 5)(2x + 4)$

   b $(2x + 3)(5x + 4)$

   c $(2x - 3)(4x + 7)$

   d $(4x - 6)(6x + 3)$

   e $(4x - 7)(2x - 2)$

   f $(3x - 7)(x - 4)$

4 Expand each of these perfect squares.

   a $(x + 3)^2$ **b** $(x + 5)^2$ **c** $(x - 4)^2$

   d $(x - 11)^2$ **e** $(2x + 3)^2$ **f** $(2 - 4x)^2$

HOMEWORK 16B

1 Expand each of the following binomial products and simplify.

   a $(a + 1)(a - 1)$

   b $(x + 3)(x - 3)$

   c $(2x + 1)(2x - 1)$

   d $(2x - y)(2x + y)$

2 A square has sides of length of x cm. The square is changed to become a rectangle by adding 1 cm to each of two opposite sides and subtracting 1 cm from each of the two perpendicular sides.
Write down an expression for the area of the rectangle.

3 A square has sides of length $3x$ cm. The square is changed to become a rectangle by adding 4 cm to each of two opposite sides and subtracting 4 cm from each of the two perpendicular sides.
Write down an expression for the area of the rectangle.

Section 2: Factorising quadratic expressions

HOMEWORK 16C

1 Copy these equations and fill in the blanks.
  a $(x + 6)(x + 8) = x^2 + \boxed{}x + \boxed{}$
  b $(x + \boxed{})(x + 6) = x^2 + 10x + \boxed{}$
  c $(x + 7)(x - \boxed{}) = x^2 - 2x - \boxed{}$
  d $(3x - 2)(x - \boxed{}) = 3x^2 - \boxed{} + 6$
  e $(\boxed{}x + \boxed{})(2x + 7) = 4x^2 + 18x + \boxed{}$

2 Find two numbers that meet each set of conditions.
  a Have a sum of 7 and a product of 12.
  b Add to give 8 and multiply to give 12.
  c Have a product of −14 and a sum of 5.
  d Multiply to give 36 and add to give −13.

3 Factorise these quadratic expressions.
  a $x^2 + 7x + 12$ b $x^2 + 5x + 4$
  c $x^2 + 11x + 30$

> **Tip**
>
> Factorising is the opposite of expanding.

4 Factorise these quadratic expressions.
  a $x^2 - 6x + 8$ b $x^2 - 6x + 5$
  c $x^2 - 8x + 12$

5 Factorise these quadratic expressions.
  a $x^2 + x - 6$ b $x^2 + 4x - 5$
  c $x^2 - 3x - 10$

6 Factorise fully.
  a $4x^2 + 8x + 3$ b $6x^2 - 7x - 3$
  c $4x^2 + 2x - 20$

HOMEWORK 16D

1 Factorise each expression.
  a $x^2 - 9$ b $x^2 - 36$ c $x^2 - 121$
  d $x^2 - 64$ e $x^2 - 1$

2 Using $(a - b)(a + b) = a^2 - b^2$, evaluate the following.
  a $80^2 - 76^2$ b $48^2 - 37^2$ c $754^2 - 749^2$
  d $57^2 - 36^2$ e $847^2 - 843^2$

3 Use the difference of two squares method to find the value of a in each triangle (**a**–**d**).
Leave the answer in square root form.

a
b

c
d

Section 3: Apply your skills

HOMEWORK 16E

1 Write an expression for the area of each of the shapes (**a**–**c**) shown below.

a
b
c

2 The cost of vinyl flooring is £21.50 per square metre.
A new office is a rectangle $x + 3$ metres by $2x - 1$ metres.
  a Write an expression for the area to be covered by the flooring.
  b Write an expression for the cost of the flooring.
  c Given that $x = 14$, find the cost of the flooring.

3 A carpet fitter has a square piece of carpet with sides of x metres.
He plans to cut a 40 cm wide strip off the square carpet and place it along the adjacent side of the square, forming a rectangle. Any carpet not required will be thrown away.
  a Express the length and breadth of the rectangular carpet in terms of x.

> **Tip**
>
> It will help to make this clear if you draw a diagram.

  b Write an expression for the area of the rectangular carpet.
  c What area of carpet has he thrown away?

4 **a** Factorise these two quadratic expressions.
 i $x^2 - 7x + 12$ **ii** $x^2 - 8x + 12$
 b Write another quadratic expression with a first term of x^2 and a constant term of 12.

5 Use $a^2 - b^2 = (a + b)(a - b)$ to evaluate $2001^2 - 1999^2$.

6 The area of a quadrilateral is expressed as $x^2 + 12x + 36$
Can this shape be a square? Give a reason for your answer.

Tip

Try factorising the expression for the area of the quadrilateral.

Chapter 16 review

1 Expand and simplify by collecting like terms.
 a $(x - 4)^2 + (x - 3)^2$ **b** $(x - 5)^2 + (x + 5)^2$

2 Copy these equations and fill in the blanks.
 a $(x + 5)(x - \square) = x^2 + 2x - \square$
 b $(x + 3)(x - \square) = x^2 - 2x - \square$
 c $(x + 3)(x - \square) = x^2 - \square$
 d $(x + 6)(\square - \square) = x^2 - x - 42$

3 Factorise the following expressions.
 a $x^2 + 5x + 4$ **b** $x^2 - 5x + 4$
 c $x^2 - 7x + 12$ **d** $x^2 - 3x - 18$

4 A rectangular field has an area of $x^2 - 8x + 12$ metres.
 a Factorise this expression.
 b Express the length and breadth of the field in terms of x.
 c Write an expression in simplest terms for the perimeter of the field.

5 Use the difference between two squares to simplify the expression $(x + 8)^2 - (x - 8)^2$

6 Write an expression in its simplest form for the area of the shaded part of the rectangle shown below.

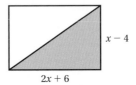

$x - 4$

$2x + 6$

7 Factorise fully.
 a $2x^2 - x - 6$ **b** $4x^2 + 2x - 12$
 c $6x^2 - 8x - 8$ **d** $4x^2 - 10x + 4$

17 Equations

Section 1: Linear equations
HOMEWORK 17A

1 Solve these equations.
 a $x + 6 = 9$ **b** $x - 5 = 12$ **c** $-3x = 18$
 d $x + 4 = 22\frac{1}{2}$ **e** $4x = -16$ **f** $5x - 21 = 9$

Tip

When solving a linear equation you are trying to find the value of the letter that will make the equation true.

2 Solve these equations.
 a $2a - 5 = 1$
 b $5b + 4 = 24$
 c $7d - 7 = 42$
 d $5e - 2 = 28$
 e $12h + 11 = 35$
 f $3x + 13 = -5$
 g $-8x - 6 = 42$
 h $7x - 52 = -87$

3 Solve these equations.
 a $2(x + 5) = 16$ **b** $4(x - 3) = 8$
 c $7(x - 2) = 21$ **d** $4(x - 3) = -20$
 e $2(x - 5) = 42$ **f** $-3(x - 4) = 27$

HOMEWORK 17B

1. Solve the following equations. Check by substitution.
   - **a** $3x - 7 = 2x + 5$
   - **b** $4x + 3 = 5x - 2$
   - **c** $5x - 6 = 6x - 17$
   - **d** $2x + 10 = 5x + 25$
   - **e** $6x - 9 = 8x + 5$
   - **f** $4x - 11 = 6x - 1$

2. Solve these equations by expanding the brackets first.
   - **a** $2(x + 4) = 11(x - 5)$
   - **b** $3(x + 3) = 6(x - 6)$
   - **c** $5(x - 2) = \frac{1}{2}(x + 7)$
   - **d** $2(x - 2) = 4(x - 4)$
   - **e** $3(x - 2) = 4(x - 1)$
   - **f** $\frac{1}{2}(x + 7) = 6(x - 4)$

3. State whether each of the following is an identity, an equation, a formula or an expression.
   - **a** $4x + 3 = 11$
   - **b** $2(x + y) = 2x + 2y$
   - **c** $3x + 6$
   - **d** $V = IR$

HOMEWORK 17C

1. For each of the following, write an equation and solve it to find the unknown number.
   - **a** Four times a certain number is 212. What is the number?
   - **b** 6 less than a number is −5. What is the number?
   - **c** 11 greater than a number is −6. What is the number?
   - **d** Three less than six times a number is 39. What is the number?
   - **e** Two consecutive numbers have a sum of 43. What are the numbers?

2. A rectangle has the side lengths $x + 4$ and $2(x - 1)$.
   - **a** Write an expression for the perimeter of the rectangle.
   - **b** Find the value of x if the perimeter is 40 cm.

3. I have three piles of stones. The second pile has twice as many stones as the first pile, and the third pile has four more stones than the second pile. Altogether I have 64 stones. How many stones are there in each pile?

4. Wilf buys 20 stamps and gets £1.60 change from £10. How much does each stamp cost?

5. Multiplying a certain number by six and adding 11 to the result gives the same answer as multiplying the number by eight and subtracting five from the result. What is the number?

Section 2: Quadratic equations
HOMEWORK 17D

1. Solve for x.
   - **a** $x^2 - 6x = 0$
   - **b** $x^2 + x = 0$
   - **c** $5x^2 + x = 0$
   - **d** $3x^2 + x = 0$

> **Tip**
>
> In a quadratic equation the largest power of a variable is squared.

2. Solve for x.
   - **a** $x^2 - 25 = 0$
   - **b** $81 - x^2 = 0$
   - **c** $9x^2 - 1 = 0$
   - **d** $4x^2 - 36 = 0$

3. Find the roots of each equation.
   - **a** $x^2 + x - 6 = 0$
   - **b** $x^2 - 7x + 12 = 0$
   - **c** $8x^2 + 10x - 3 = 0$
   - **d** $18x^2 - 6x - 4 = 0$

4. Solve these equations.
   - **a** $x^2 + 6x = -8$
   - **b** $x^2 + 3x = 10$
   - **c** $x^2 - 2x - 2 = 13$
   - **d** $x^2 - 6x = -8$
   - **e** $6x^2 + 7x = -2$
   - **f** $5x^2 - 9x + 1 = 3$

HOMEWORK 17E

1. Form an equation and solve it to find the unknown numbers.
   - **a** The product of a certain positive whole number and three more than that number is 270. What could the number be?
   - **b** The product of a certain positive whole number and five less than that number is 126. What could the number be?
   - **c** The difference between the square of a number and twice the original number is 8. What are possible values of the number?
   - **d** The product of two consecutive positive even numbers is 168. What are the numbers?

2. A rectangular field has an area of 1575 m². The length of the field is 10 m longer than the width of the field. Form an equation and solve it to find the length and width of the field.

3. The base of a triangle is 6 cm longer than twice its height. If the area of the triangle is 54 cm², what is its height?

Section 3: Simultaneous equations
HOMEWORK 17F

1 Solve the following pairs of simultaneous equations by substitution.

a $x + y = 3$
   $2x + y = 4$

b $x - y = 4$
   $3x + y = 8$

c $x + y = 2$
   $3x - y = 14$

d $3x + 2y = 23$
   $x - 2y = 1$

e $2x + 2y = 6$
   $2x + y = 0$

f $3x + y = 12$
   $2x - y = 18$

> **Tip**
>
> Simultaneous equations have the same solution. The solution **must** satisfy both equations.

2 Solve these simultaneous equations.

a $2x + y = 10$
   $3x + 2y = 16$

b $3x + 2y = -4$
   $x - 2y = 12$

c $5x + 2y = -11$
   $6x - 2y = 0$

d $-3x + 2y = -13$
   $3x + 4y = 37$

e $3x + 2y = -33$
   $4x - 4y = -24$

f $5x - 3y = 2$
   $4x - 6y = -20$

HOMEWORK 17G

1 Solve the following pairs of simultaneous equations by elimination.

a $2x + 3y = -13$
   $4x - 2y = -50$

b $3x + y = -37$
   $5x - 4y = -22$

c $3x + 5y = 37$
   $4x + 2y = 26$

d $6x - 2y = 28$
   $4x - 3y = 32$

e $3x + 4y = 39$
   $9x + 3y = 36$

f $5x - 4y = -32$
   $4x + 5y = 40$

2 Solve each pair of simultaneous equations. Choose the most suitable method for doing this.

a $x + y = 0$
   $3x + 2y = 2$

b $2x - y = 3$
   $4x + y = 21$

c $3x + 2y = -3$
   $2x - 3y = -24$

d $x - 3y = 10$
   $2x + y = -1$

e $6x + 2y = -28$
   $2x - 3y = -2$

f $5x + 8y = -2$
   $6x - 3y = 48$

HOMEWORK 17H

1 Ben and Molly buy their friends drinks at the café.
Ben bought three shakes and two coffees for £10.20. Molly bought four shakes and one coffee for £10.35.
How much are:
a shakes?   b coffees?

2 Shazan is counting the money in her till. She has 37 notes, some of which are £5 and some £10, making a total of £280. How many of each note does she have?

3 Two numbers have a sum of 62 and a difference of 24. What are the numbers?

4 The sum of two numbers, x and y, is 80. When $2y$ is subtracted from $5x$, the result is 99. Find the value of x and y.

5 A plumber charges a call-out fee plus an amount per hour. A job taking five hours costs £155 and a job taking three and a half hours costs £117.50. How much would a job taking eight hours cost?

Section 4: Using graphs to solve equations
HOMEWORK 17I

1 The graph shown below represents a cyclist's training session

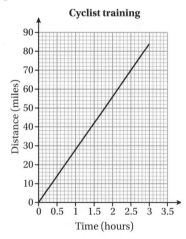

a Use the graph to estimate how far the cyclist has travelled after two hours.
b How long did it take the cyclist to cover a distance of 42 miles?

The equation $s = \dfrac{d}{t}$ can be used to work out the speed (s) of the cyclist.

c Use values for d and t from the graph to work out the speed at which this cyclist was travelling.

2 Use the graph of the equation $y = 4x - 3$ shown below to find the value of y for the following values of x.

a $x = 0$
b $x = 2$
c $x = 1$

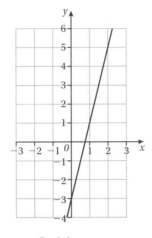

3 The graph below shows how water drains from a tank at a constant rate.

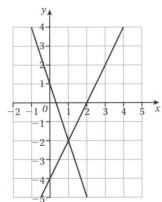

Draining water

a How much water was in the tank to start with?
b How much water was left in the tank after six minutes?
c What is the equation of the graph?

4 The graph below shows two linear equations $y = 2x - 4$ and $y = -3x + 1$. Use the graph to find the solution to the two equations.

5 The graph of the quadratic equation shown below models the path of a ball thrown up into the air.

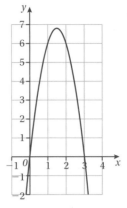

a What do you think the axes represent in this case?
b What does the y value of 0 represent?
c Are values of $y < 0$ meaningless in this context?
d Use the graph to give information about the maximum height of the ball.

6 The graph below shows the equation $y = x^2 + 3x - 6$

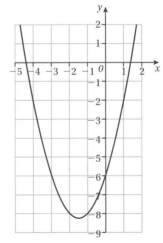

Use the graph to find approximate solutions to the equation $x^2 + 3x - 6 = 0$

Chapter 17 review

1 Solve for x.
a $6x - 2 = 4(2x - 3)$ b $x^2 = 15 - 2x$
c $4(x - 3) = 3(x + 12)$ d $-x^2 = 8x + 12$
e $(x + 3)^2 = 49$ f $(x + 5)(x + 2) = 10$

2 Study the graph shown below.

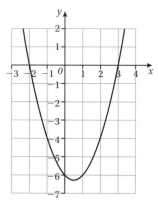

a What are the roots of the quadratic equation modelled by this graph?

3 Frank thinks that $y = 2x + 4$ is equivalent to $y = 4x + 8$. Is he correct? Give two reasons for your answer.

4 Give a reason why the equations $2x + y = 6$ and $2x + y = 8$ are not simultaneous equations.

5 If you drew the graph of $y = x^2 + 2x$ where would the curve cut the x–axis?

6 The sum of two numbers is 28 and their difference is 6.
a Write a set of equations in terms of x and y to show this.
b Solve the equations simultaneously to find the two numbers.

18 Functions and sequences

Section 1: Sequences and patterns
HOMEWORK 18A

1 Find the next three terms in each sequence and describe the rule you used to find them.
a 11, 13, 15, ...   b 88, 99, 110, ...
c 64, 32, 16, ...   d 8, 16, 32, ...
e −2, −4, −6, −8, ...   f $\frac{1}{4}, \frac{1}{2}, 1, ...$
g 1, 2, 4, 7, ...   h 1, 6, 11, 16, ...

2 List the first four terms of the sequences that follow these rules.
a Start with seven and add two each time.
b Start with 37 and subtract five each time.
c Start with one and multiply by $\frac{1}{2}$ each time.
d Start with five then multiply by two and add one each time.
e Start with 100, divide by two and subtract three each time.

Tip

Look at how the numbers change each time. Is the change the same?

3 Josh skims a stone across a pond. Each 'bounce' is $\frac{2}{3}$ the length of the previous one.
a If the first bounce is 216 cm, how long will the fourth bounce be?
b How many times will the stone bounce before the bounce is less than 1 cm long?

Section 2: Finding the nth term
HOMEWORK 18B

1 The nth term of a sequence is $n - 2$. Write down the first 10 terms of the sequence.

2 Write down the first 10 terms of the sequences that have the following nth term rules.
a $n + 4$ b $4n$ c $n - 7$ d $\frac{n}{3}$ e $2n + 1$

3 What sequences would be created by putting the numbers −5 to 5 in order using the following rules:
a $3n$ b $2n + 3$ c $3n - 4$
d $2n + \frac{1}{4}$ e $\frac{n}{2} - 1$

4 Find the expression for the nth term in the sequence that begins 5, 9, 13, 17, ...

5 Find the expressions for the nth term in the following sequences.

   a   3, 5, 7, 9, ...   **b**   3, 7, 11, 15, ...

   c   −1, 4, 9, 14, ...   **d**   7, 12, 17, 22, ...

   e   −3, 0, 3, 6, ...   **f**   −1, 6, 13, 20, ...

Tip

Start by finding the difference between the terms.

6 Bonita is conducting an experiment in science and gets the following pattern of results:

53, 61, 69, 77, ...

Write an expression for the nth term for Bonita's results.

7 Consider the sequence: 2, 10, 18, 26, 34, 42, 50, ...

   a Find the nth term of the sequence.

   b Find the 200th term.

   c Which term of this sequence has the value 234? Show full working.

   d Show that 139 is not a term in the sequence.

8 For each sequence below find the general term and the 50th term.

   a   7, 9, 11, 13, ...   **b**   −5, −13, −21, −29, ...

   c   2, 8, 14, 20, 26, ...   **d**   4, 9, 16, 25, ...

   e   2.3, 3.5, 4.7, 5.9, ...

Section 3: Functions
HOMEWORK 18C

1 Complete the table for each of the given position-to-term rules.

Position-to-term rule	1st term	2nd term	3rd term	4th term	10th term	50th term	100th term
$3n + 6$							
$5n − 4$							
$7n + 3$							
$6n − \frac{1}{2}$							
$\frac{n}{4} + 2$							
$−3n + 5$							

Tip

Substitute position values into the rule to find each term.

2 Ben has ten rectangular tables in his classroom that can seat six people; two along each side and one at each of the ends as shown in the diagram below.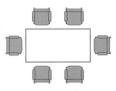

   a What different numbers of people can he seat if he pushes the tables together with the long sides touching?

   b What different numbers of people can he seat if he pushes the tables together with the ends together?

3 The number of minutes needed to cook a turkey is given by the expression $40m + 20$, where m is the mass of the turkey in kg. Construct a table to show the cooking time for turkeys ranging from 3 kg to 15 kg.

Section 4: Special sequences
HOMEWORK 18D

1 If a cow produces its first female calf at age two years and after that produces another single female calf every year, how many female calves are there after 12 years, assuming none die and that each cow produces calves in the same way?

2 Write down the sequence of the first 12 triangle numbers, with each term doubled.

3   **a** Write down the first 10 square numbers.

   b Write down the first five cube numbers.

4   **a** Following the rules for the Fibonacci series, but starting with the numbers −5 and 3, write down the first ten terms of the sequence.

   b Following the same rule, start the sequence with the numbers 3 and −5. Write down the first ten terms of the sequence. Does this generate the same sequence?

5 The 7th and 8th terms of a sequence formed using the Fibonacci rule are −14 and −23. What are the first two terms?

6 Write down the first ten terms of the sequence formed by using the rule $2n^2 - n$.

7 Write down the first ten terms of the sequence formed by $\dfrac{(n^2 + n)}{2}$

What is the name given to this sequence?

Chapter 18 review

1 A new bacteria is growing in a laboratory. After one hour it consists of 10 cells. There are 16 after two hours, 22 after three hours and 28 after four hours.
  a If it continues to grow the same rate, how many cells will there be after 24 hours?
  b Find an expression that will work out the number of cells after any number of hours.

2 The number of rats on an island is recorded each month.
After one month there are eight rats.
After two months there are 20 rats.
After three months there are 32 rats.
  a If the population keeps growing at the same rate, and no rats die, how many rats will there be at the end of the year?
  b Give a reason why a sequence of this type is unlikely to work in reality.

3 A basketball is dropped from a height of 16 m. For each bounce the ball returns to $\dfrac{3}{4}$ of the height of the previous bounce. How high will the fifth bounce be? Give your answer to the nearest centimetre.

4 What sequences would be created by putting the numbers 1 to 10 in order into the following functions?
  a $f(x) = 3 + x$ **b** $f(x) = -2x$
  c $f(x) = 6 - x$ **d** $f(x) = \dfrac{x}{4}$
  e $f(x) = 3x - 1$

5 For the sequence $2n - 3$, write down:
  a the first five terms
  b the 10th term
  c the 25th term.

6 Find the expressions for the nth term in the following sequences.
  a 4, 6, 8, 10, ...   **b** 5, 9, 13, 17, ...
  c −2, 1, 4, 7, ...   **d** 2, 7, 12, 17, ...

7 Write down the first ten terms of the sequence with the nth term $\dfrac{(n^2 + 1)}{2}$

19 Basic probability

Section 1: The probability scale
HOMEWORK 19A

1 In an experiment, one student rolled a dice 36 times and another rolled the dice 480 times. The outcome of each experiment was summarised in a table.

Experiment A

Possible outcomes	1	2	3	4	5	6
Frequency	7	6	4	6	5	8

Experiment B

Possible outcomes	1	2	3	4	5	6
Frequency	80	78	84	78	76	84

  a Does Experiment A suggest that you will get a 6 twice as often as a 3 when you roll the dice? Give a reason for your answer.
  b If student A rolled the dice another 36 times, how many more 6s would you expect her to get? Why?
  c The probability of rolling any number on an unbiased dice is $\dfrac{1}{6}$. Do the results of the experiments show this? Give a reason for your answer.
  d If you did Experiment B, what results would you expect? Why?
  e If the student who did Experiment B rolled the dice another 480 times would you expect the frequencies of each number to double? Give a reason why or why not.

2 An A & E at a large hospital treats 1200 patients per week. A sample of 50 patients showed that 27 were male.

a What percentage of the sample was female?

b How many of the 1200 patients would you expect to be male? Why?

3 Nadia made a spinner with green, red and black sectors. When she spun it 200 times she found it landed on green 60 times, on red 80 times and on black 60 times.

a Draw a diagram to show what the spinner is likely to look like.

b What is the probability that the spinner will land on red?

4 Research has shown the probability of a person being left-handed is 0.11. How many left-handed people would you expect to find in a population of 20 000?

5 In a sample of 100 drivers passing through a village, 17 were found to be speeding. Express this as a probability.

6 Salma has a bag containing one red, one white and one green ball.

Red													
White																
Green															

She draws a ball at random and replaces it before drawing again. She does this 50 times. She uses a tally table, as shown below, to record the outcomes of her experiment.

a Calculate the relative frequency of drawing each colour.

b Express her chance of drawing a red ball as a percentage.

c What is the sum of the three relative frequencies?

d What should your chances be in theory of drawing each colour?

Section 2: Calculating probability
HOMEWORK 19B

1 An unbiased six-sided dice with the numbers 1 to 6 on the faces is rolled.

a What are the possible outcomes of this event?

b Calculate the probability of rolling a prime number.

c What is the probability of rolling an even number?

d What is the probability of rolling a number greater than seven?

2 Sally has ten identical cards numbered 1 to 10. She draws a card at random and records the number on it.

a What are the possible outcomes for this event?

b Calculate the probability that Sally will draw:

  i the number 5

  ii any one of the ten numbers

  iii a multiple of three

  iv a number < 4

  v a number < 5

  vi a number < 6

3 There are five cups of coffee on a tray. Two of them contain sugar.

a What are your chances of choosing a cup with sugar in it?

b Which choice would you expect? Why?

4 A dartboard is divided into 20 sectors numbered from 1 to 20. If a dart is equally likely to land in any of these sectors, calculate:

a P(<8)   b P(odd)

c P(prime)   d P(multiple of 3)

e P(multiple of 5).

5 A school has 40 classrooms numbered from 1 to 40. The number of one of the classrooms is picked at random. Work out the probability that a classroom number picked has the digit 1 in it.

Section 3: Experimental probability
HOMEWORK 19C

1 a The table below shows two possible outcomes when a six-sided dice is rolled. Copy and complete this table using the information in parts b and c.

Possible outcomes	Predicted frequency	Actual frequency
odd number		
even number		

b Predict how many times you think each outcome will occur in 60 rolls of the dice. Write your predictions in the table.

c Graham rolled the dice 60 times and recorded the following outcomes.

5	6	3	2	1	3	6	3	2	3	3	4
1	2	4	6	6	6	5	1	6	2	5	5
3	3	1	4	5	2	2	4	2	6	4	6
2	6	1	5	6	3	5	6	5	4	1	4
1	2	5	4	1	1	4	4	2	5	4	3

Use this information to write in the actual frequencies in the table.

d How do Graham's results compare with your predictions?

e How many times would you expect an even number to show if you rolled this dice 3000 times? Give reasons for your answer.

HOMEWORK 19D

1 The probability that a driver is speeding on a stretch of road is 0.27. What is the probability that a driver is not speeding?

2 For a fly-fishing competition, the organisers place 45 trout, 30 salmon and 15 pike in a small lake.

a What is the probability that the first fish caught is a salmon?

b If the first fish caught is a pike and it is not replaced, what is the probability that the second fish caught is also a pike?

c Joanne gets a turn to fish after two trout, four salmon and a pike have been caught and not replaced. Does she have more than a 50% chance that the first fish she catches is a trout? Write down how you worked out your answer.

3 Below is a list of six possible outcomes when a person is chosen at random from a large group. Say whether each of the following pairs of outcomes (**a–g**) are mutually exclusive or not.
Outcome A: the person is female
Outcome B: the person is male
Outcome C: the person is under 18
Outcome D: the person is over 21
Outcome E: the person has a driver's licence
Outcome F: the person is multilingual

a Outcomes A and B   **b** Outcomes A and C
c Outcomes C and D   **d** Outcomes D and F
e Outcomes E and D   **f** Outcomes A and E
g Outcomes C and F

4 In the situation in question 3, what is the maximum number of outcomes that could be met when one person is drawn at random from the crowd? Give a reason for your answer.

5 Andy has 1200 songs on his music player. 480 are heavy metal, 240 are drum and bass and the rest are pop.

a If he puts the player on random play, what are the chances that the first song played will be a pop song?

b What is the probability that a random song will not be heavy metal?

HOMEWORK 19E

1 The number of students who do and do not wear glasses or contact lenses is recorded in the table.

Gender	Wear glasses or contact lenses	Don't wear glasses or contact lenses
Female	116	464
Male	92	328

a Draw a frequency tree to show this data.

b What percentage of female students wear glasses or contact lenses?

c In a group of 100 mixed male and female students, how many would you expect to be wearing glasses or contact lenses?

2 In January, the weather service forecast snow on 10 days of the month and no snow on the other days. It did not snow on one of the days when snow was forecast and it snowed twice on days when no snow was forecast.

a Draw a frequency tree to show this information.

b Milla says the weather forecast was accurate 90% of the time. Is she correct? Give reasons for your answer.

3 In a survey of 250 teenagers who use online social media sites, 195 students said they were sure their passwords were secure. The others answered that they were not sure. Of those who felt their passwords were secure 92 passwords were considered non-secure. Of those who were not sure, 32 had secure passwords.

a Show the results of this survey on a frequency tree.

b What percentage of students had secure passwords?

c What percentage of students who thought their passwords were secure actually had non-secure passwords?

4 In a global survey of 4400 parents of 14–17 year olds, 44% of parents admitted that they spied on their children's social media accounts. Of this sample, 10% of the parents were British and 264 of them said they spied on their children's accounts. Of the rest of the parents, 2288 said they did not spy on their children's accounts.

   a Draw a frequency tree to show the information.

   b Comment on the data for British parents compared to the sample as a whole.

Section 4: Mixed probability problems
HOMEWORK 19F

1 In an opinion poll, 5000 teenagers were asked what make of mobile phone they would choose from four options (A, B, C or D). The probability of choosing each option is given in the table.

Phone	A	B	C	D
P(Option)	0.36	0.12	0.4	

   a Calculate P(D).   **b** What is P(*not* D)?

   c What is the probability a teenager would choose either B or D?

   d How many teenagers in a group of 1000 would you expect to choose Option C if these probabilities are correct?

2 Mina's dad is told by his doctor that his risk of getting heart disease in the next five years is 14.6%.

   a Do you think Mina's dad is likely or unlikely to get heart disease? Why?

   b In a group of 250 people with the same risk factors as Mina's dad, how many would you expect to get heart disease in the next five years?

3 In a car park there are 35 red, 42 white, 12 black and 29 silver cars. 24 parking spaces are empty. What is the probability that a parking space chosen at random will contain:

   a a red car?   **b** a silver car?

   c not a black car?   **d** no car at all?

4 Draw unbiased spinners that will land on blue, with the following probabilities.

   a $P(\text{blue}) = \frac{1}{6}$, $P(\text{red}) = \frac{5}{6}$

   b $P(\text{blue}) = \frac{1}{3}$, $P(\text{white}) = \frac{1}{3}$, $P(\text{black}) = \frac{1}{3}$

   c $P(not\ \text{blue}) = \frac{1}{8}$

   d $P(\text{black}) = \frac{4}{5}$, $P(\text{blue}) = P(not\ \text{black})$.

5 A company has 1800 employees. Of those, 6% use illegal substances. The company tests all employees for illegal substances and finds that 1% of the users test negative and 1% of the non-users test positive.

   a Draw up a two-way table to show this information using actual numbers of employees.

   b Draw a frequency tree to show the data.

Chapter 19 review

1 Mia has a spinner divided into four equal sectors coloured red, yellow, green and blues.

   a If Mia spins the spinner 80 times, how many times would you expect it to land on blue? Why?

   b Mia finds that the spinner lands on blue 17 times in the 80 trials. Comment on what this result shows.

2 The table shows the actual frequency of each number on a dice in an experiment.

Outcome	Frequency in 120 trials	Relative frequency
1	16	
2	22	
3	16	
4	24	
5	24	
6	18	
odd		
even		
> 3		
< 5		

   a Use the information in the table to calculate the relative frequency of getting each number from 1 to 6. Give your answer as a decimal to two places.

   b Work out the actual frequency of odd, even, > 3 and < 5 from the data given.

   c Which of these four events has the highest relative frequency?

   d If you rolled the same dice another 60 times, how many times would you expect to get a result < 5? Show how you worked out your answer.

3 The frequency tree below shows the results of a test to see whether people are allergic to cat hair.

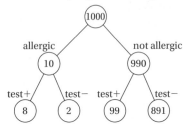

a What percentage of people are allergic to cat hair?

b What percentage of people test positive for the allergy?

c What percentage of people with a positive test result are actually allergic to cat hair?

d If a group of 50 people tested positive for cat hair allergy, how many would you expect to be allergic to cat hair?

e Based on these test results, what is the likelihood that a person who tests negatively for cat hair is actually allergic to cat hair?

4 An educational authority produces the frequency tree shown below based on research done with GCSE students.

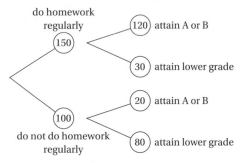

a How many students are in the sample?

b What percentage of students do homework regularly?

c What percentage of students who don't do homework regularly manage to get an A or B grade?

d In a class of 40 students, how many would you expect to attain a lower grade if they fall into the group that:

　i does homework regularly?

　ii doesn't do homework regularly?

e What does this frequency diagram suggest?

20 3D objects

Section 1: 3D objects and their nets
HOMEWORK 20A

1 What shape or shapes are the faces of each of the following solids?

a Cube

b Pentagonal-based pyramid

c Pentagonal prism

d Cylinder

e Trapezoidal prism

2 Copy and complete the following by filling in appropriate words or phrases.

The net of a solid is a _____ drawing that shows how the _____ of the solid are joined to each other so that they can be folded up into a solid. You can form a 3D object by _____ the net along the _____ .

When you draw the net of a solid, you need to think about: how many _____ it has, what _____ the faces are, and how the faces are _____ .

3 Sketch a possible net for each of the solids (**a–d**) shown.

a

b

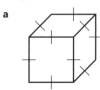

c

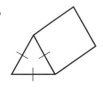

d

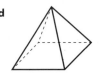

4 Draw an accurate net of the cuboid shown below and use it to build a model of the object.

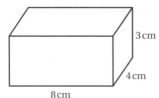

3 cm
4 cm
8 cm

Section 2: Drawing 3D objects
HOMEWORK 20B

1 Copy and complete the diagrams shown below to indicate the hidden edges of the solids (**a**–**d**).

a   **b**

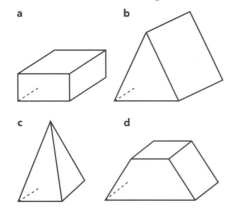

c   **d**

2 Draw the solids (**a** and **b**) on centimetre squared grid paper. The dimensions are given in centimetres.

a   **b**

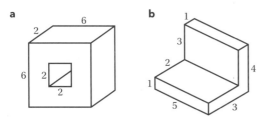

3 Draw the shapes (**a**–**c**) shown below on isometric grid paper. The dimensions are given as distances between the dots on the paper.

a   **b**   **c**

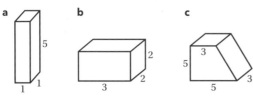

4 Assuming no blocks are missing, how many blocks would you need to build the solids (**a** and **b**) shown below?

a   **b**

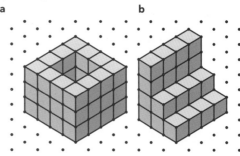

5 A prism has a cross-section in the shape of an isosceles triangle with a base of 6 cm and a height of 4 cm. The distance between the triangular end faces is 8 cm.
 a Draw this 3D object without using a grid.
 b Label the diagram to show the dimensions.
 c Sketch a possible net of the object.

6 Redraw the solids (**a** and **b**) shown below on an isometric grid indicating what they would look like if the blocks marked with an X were removed from each shape.

a   **b**

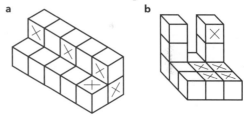

Section 3: Plan and elevation views
HOMEWORK 20C

1 Sketch each of the following objects as they would appear in a plan view and a front elevation.
 a A box of cereal   **b** A can of food
 c Your desk

2 Draw a plan view, front elevation and side elevation from the right of the solids (**a**–**c**) shown below.

a   **b**   **c**

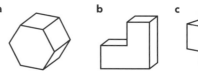

3 Draw the plan, front and right-hand views of the building shown below.

Chapter 20 review

1 Sketch and label the net of:
- **a** a cube with edges 4 cm long
- **b** a cuboid with a square face of side 2 cm and a length of 4 cm.

2 The solid shown below has been drawn on a squared grid. Redraw it on an isometric grid.

3
- **a** Draw the solid shown below on an isometric grid. Show the hidden edges on your diagram.
- **b** Draw the plan view, front elevation and right-hand side elevation of this solid.

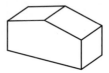

4 A view of a public library building is shown below. Draw the plan, front and side elevations of the building.

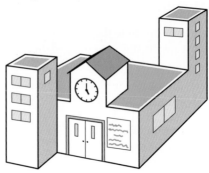

21 Units and measure

Section 1: Standard units of measurement

HOMEWORK 21A

1 Convert the following lengths and masses into the given units.
- **a** 3.6 km = ☐ m
- **b** 45 cm = ☐ mm
- **c** 76 m = ☐ mm
- **d** 2.7 m = ☐ mm
- **e** 0.04 m = ☐ cm
- **f** 6.23 kg = ☐ g

Tip

When converting between metric units if the unit is bigger, divide by the conversion factor. If the unit is smaller, multiply by the conversion factor.

2 Add the following capacities. Give your answers in the units indicated in brackets.
- **a** 2.6 l + 6 l (ml)
- **b** 5.1 l + 320 ml (l)
- **c** 25 l + 3.6 l + 925 ml (l)

3 Convert the following lengths and masses into the given units.

a Total mass in kilograms of five bags of sultanas, each of mass 700 g.

b The length in centimetres of a 6.34 m long bus.

c 3472 kg of scrap metal in tonnes.

HOMEWORK 21B

1 A 10 km run starts at 10:45:00. The winning time is 37 minutes and 38 seconds.

a At what time does the winner cross the line?

b The runner who comes second crosses the line in 38 minutes and 5 seconds. How far behind the winner is she?

c The third-placed runner finishes a further 36 seconds behind. At what time does she cross the finishing line?

2 Hannah has a baby at 2.35 pm on the 8th March 2013. Calculate the baby's age at the same time on the 14th February 2014 in:

a weeks   **b** days

c hours   **d** seconds.

3 The table below shows the value of the pound against four other currencies in August 2014.

British pound (£)	1
Euro (€)	1.25
US dollar ($)	1.67
Australian dollar (AU$)	1.79
Indian rupee (Rs)	101.88

a Calculate the value of each of the other currencies in pounds at this rate (to the nearest penny).

b Convert £175 to US dollars.

c How many Indian rupees would you get if you converted £65 at this rate?

d Dilshaad has 9000 Indian rupees. What is this worth in pounds at this rate?

Tip

If £1 = $1.75, then $1 is worth
1 ÷ 1.75 pounds.

4 A plot of grass with an area of 225 000 m² needs to be seeded. 20 g of grass seed is sufficient to seed one square metre. How many kilograms of seed are needed for the whole area?

5 Convert each of the following into the required units.

a Area of 32 m² into mm²

b 77.46 m³ of cement into cm³

c Engine capacity of 1295 cm³ into litres (to the nearest 0.1 litre)

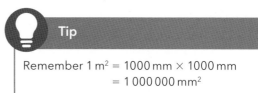

Tip

Remember 1 m² = 1000 mm × 1000 mm
= 1 000 000 mm²

Section 2: Compound units of measurement
HOMEWORK 21C

Tip

Compound measures have more than one unit of measurement, like miles per hour or pence per gram.

1 Henri earns £7.85 per hour. One week he worked 37.5 hours.
Sian earned £196.35 for working 21 hours. How much more does Sian earn per hour than Henri?

2 A plasterer can plaster an area of 45 m² in $4\frac{1}{2}$ hours. On average, what area can she plaster in 15 minutes?

3 Jake runs 42 km in 3 hours and 12 minutes. What is his average speed?

4 A car travels 504 km at an average speed of 96 km/hour. How long does this journey take?

5 Paralympian Jonnie Peacock won the 100 m at the London Paralympics in 2012 with a time of 10.9 seconds.

a Express this speed in metres per second. Give your answer to three significant figures.

b How fast is this in kilometres per hour? Give your answer to the nearest whole number.

>
> ### Tip
> Think about how many metres make a kilometre and how many seconds make an hour.

HOMEWORK 21D

1. A cuboid of material with side lengths 10 cm, 20 cm and 30 cm has a mass of 0.534 kg. Calculate the density of the material in g/cm³.

2. Calculate the volume (in cm³) of a piece of wood with a mass of 0.275 kg and a density of 0.9 g/cm³.

3. A bus exerts a force of 86 000 N on the road, spread evenly over its six tyres. Each of the six tyres has an area of 0.15 m² in contact with the road. What pressure does the bus exert on the road through each tyre?

4. A metal block has a weight of 220 000 N. The block is a cuboid with sides 100 cm, 150 cm and 175 cm long. Calculate the pressure exerted by the block in N/m² when each of the three sides is in contact with the floor.

Section 3: Maps, scale drawings and bearings
HOMEWORK 21E

1. Work out the real distance (in kilometres) that a map distance of 72 mm would represent for each scale.
   a 1 : 100   **b** 1 : 1500   **c** 1 : 18 000
   d 1 : 100 000   **e** 1 : 2 000 000

>
> ### Tip
> Scales are a way of representing big distances on smaller maps and diagrams. A scale of 1 : 100 means 1 unit is being used to represent 100 units in reality.

2. Arshwin says that a map drawn to a scale of 1 : 20 000 is a larger scale map than one drawn to 1 : 200 000. Is he correct? Give a reason for your answer.

3. The map below shows several cities.

Scale: 1 : 10 000 000

The line on the map shows the flight path of a plane flying from Norwich to Liverpool. The flight took 45 minutes.
   a Calculate the distance flown in kilometres.
   b What was the plane's average speed on this flight?

4. Toy cars are manufactured using a scale of 1 : 43. Work out:
   a the height of a car if the model is 3.2 cm high
   b the length of a car if the model is 9.7 cm long
   c the length of the model if the real length is 4.5 m.

HOMEWORK 21F

1. A garden in a new house is 55 m long and 12 m wide. Draw scaled diagrams to show what it would look like at each of these scales.
   a 1 : 200   **b** 1 : 500   **c** 1 : 750.

2. An architect is drawing a plan of a house to a scale of 1 : 50.
   a What should the scaled dimensions of the kitchen be if the real dimensions are 5900 mm by 3600 mm?
   b Calculate the scaled length of the kitchen island if it is 1.6 metres long in reality.

HOMEWORK 21G

1 Write the three-figure bearing that corresponds to each direction.
   a Due east   **b** South-west   **c** North-west

2 Use a protractor to measure the bearing of each 'plane' from base shown on the diagram below.

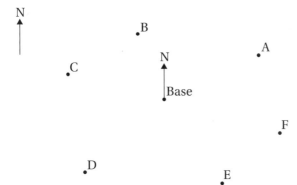

Chapter 21 review

1 Work out the following.
   a The number of seconds in 4 days.
   b The number of kilometres travelled in $5\frac{1}{2}$ hours by a car travelling at 67 km/hour.
   c The distance in km in real life of a length of 7.5 cm on a map with a scale of $1:20\,000$.
   d The number of litres in 525 000 millilitres.
   e The capacity in litres of a fish tank that is $50\,\text{cm} \times 25\,\text{cm} \times 40\,\text{cm}$.

2 The distance between London and Edinburgh is 535 km. How far would this be on a map scale of $1:2\,000\,000$?

3 Convert 75 000 cm² into m².

4 How many mm² are there in 5 m²?

5 A cyclist is travelling at an average speed of 30 km/hour for two hours on a bearing of 075°. Draw a scale diagram to show this journey using a scale of 1 cm to 10 km.

6 The density of an object is 12 kg/m³. Work out the mass of 35 m³ of the object.

7 A yacht sails due east from point A for 20 km to reach a buoy at point B. The yacht then travels 12 km on a bearing of 225° from B to reach a buoy at point C.
   a Use a scale of 1 cm to 2 km to represent this journey on a scale diagram.
   b Find the bearing from C to A.
   c Find the direct distance from C to A in kilometres.
   d If it took the yacht $1\frac{1}{4}$ hours to sail back directly from C to A, find the yacht's average speed:
     i in km/hour
     ii in m/s.

22 Formulae

Section 1: Writing formulae
HOMEWORK 22A

1 Write a formula for each statement.
   a The area of a triangle is half the product of its base length and perpendicular height.
   b To find the mean (m) of three numbers, you divide their sum by 3.
   c The volume of a cube is found by multiplying the length of an edge by itself and then by itself again.

Tip

When you write a formula always say what the variables represent.

2 A photocopy shop charges a £2.50 service fee and £0.12 per page for bulk photocopying.
  a Write a formula for the total cost £C of a photocopying job with n pages.
  b The shop decides to increase the service fee to £2.80 and drop the cost per page by 2p per page. Write a revised formula for finding the total cost.
  c In the formula £$C = 1.50 + 3n$, identify the subject of the formula, the constant and any variables in the formula.

Section 2: Substituting values into formulae
HOMEWORK 22B

1 The formula for finding the area A of a triangle is $A = \frac{1}{2}bh$, where b is the length of the base and h is the perpendicular height of the triangle. Find the area of a triangle if:
  a the base is 12 cm and the height is 9 cm
  b the base is 2.5 m and the height is 1.5 m.

2 **a** $M = 9ab$. Find M when $a = 7$ and $b = 10$.
  b $V - rs = 2uw$. Find V when $r = 8$, $s = 4$, $u = 6$ and $w = 1$.
  c $\frac{V}{30} = h$. Find V when $h = 25$.
  d $P - y = x^2$. Find P when $x = 2$ and $y = 8$.

Section 3: Changing the subject of a formula
HOMEWORK 22C

1 Make m the subject of $D = km$

2 Make c the subject of $y = mx + c$

3 Given that $P = ab - c$, make b the subject of the formula.

4 Given that $a = bx + c$, make b the subject of the formula.

Section 4: Working with formulae
HOMEWORK 22D

1 The perimeter of a rectangle can be given as $P = 2(l + b)$, where P is the perimeter, l is the length and b is the breadth.

a Make b the subject of the formula.
b Find b if the rectangle has a length of 45 cm and a perimeter of 161 cm.

Tip

When you are given shape problems it is helpful to draw a diagram and label it to show what the parts of the formula represent.

2 The circumference of a circle can be found using the formula $C = 2\pi r$, where r is the radius of the circle.
  a Make r the subject of the formula.
  b Find the radius of a circle of circumference 56.52 cm. Use $\pi = 3.14$.
  c Find the diameter of a circle of circumference 144.44 cm. Use $\pi = 3.14$.

Tip

When you are given a value for π you must use the given value to get full marks. Using a different value, for example from your calculator, can lead to rounding differences.

3 To convert temperatures from Celsius to Fahrenheit you can use the formula $F = 1.8C + 32$, where F is the temperature in degrees Fahrenheit (°F) and C is the temperature in degrees Celsius (°C). Rearrange the formula to convert from Fahrenheit to Celsius, i.e. make C the subject.

4 Using the formula above, convert:
  a 15 °C to °F
  b 92 °F to °C
  c 12 °F to °C
  d −6 °C to °F

5 Normal adult body temperature is about 37 °C. What is this in Farenheit?

6 Water boils at 100 °C at sea level. What is the Fahrenheit equivalent of that temperature?

7 The lowest temperature ever recorded on Earth was −129 °F (in Antarctica). What is this in °C?

Chapter 22 review

1. Change the subject of each formula to the letter given in square brackets.

   a $v = u + at$ [t]   **b** $s = x + y + z$ [y]

   c $fh = g$ [f]   **d** $ab + c = d$ [a]

   e $\dfrac{x}{y} = z$ [x]   **f** $y = x - 3$ [x]

   g $S = \dfrac{D}{T}$ [D]   **h** $\dfrac{x}{y} = \dfrac{m}{n}$ [m]

   i $a - \dfrac{b}{c} = x$ [b]   **j** $\sqrt{x} = y$ [x]

   k $\sqrt{xy} = z$ [y]   **l** $x\sqrt{y} = a$ [y]

   m $\sqrt{x} + y = m$ [x]   **n** $\sqrt{x} - y = b$ [y]

   o $y\sqrt{x} = m$ [x]   **p** $\dfrac{x}{y} = \dfrac{p}{q}$ [y]

2. Given $I = \dfrac{E}{R}$, find I when $E = 250$ and $R = 125$.

3. $P = \dfrac{t - m}{d}$. If $P = 12$, $t = 16$ and $m = 8$, what is d?

4. **a** $y = \dfrac{12}{x} + 2$. Find y when $x = -3$.

   b $y = (x + 3)(x - 1)$. Find x when $y = -3$.

   c $y = 2^x$. Find y when $x = -4$.

5. The formula $d = \dfrac{v}{10} + 2$ can be used to work out how many car lengths you should leave between you and the car in front of you when you are driving at v km/h.

   a How many car lengths should you leave between you and the car in front of you when you are travelling at 100 km/h?

   b If you are obeying this rule and you have left 7.5 car lengths space in front of you, what is your speed?

23 Volume and surface area

Section 1: Prisms and cylinders

HOMEWORK 23A

Give your answers to three significant figures where appropriate.

1. Calculate the volume of each of the solid prisms (**a**–**h**) shown.

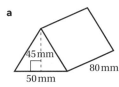

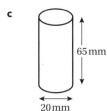

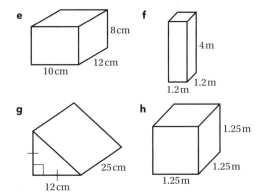

2. A pocket dictionary is 14 cm long, 9.5 cm wide and 2.5 cm thick. Calculate the volume it takes up.

3. A wooden cube has six identical faces each of area 64 cm².

   a What is the total surface area of the cube?

   b What is the height of the cube?

4 A teacher is ordering wooden blocks to use in her maths classroom. The blocks are cuboids with dimensions 10 cm × 8 cm × 5 cm.
   a Calculate the surface area of one block.
   b The teacher needs 450 blocks. What is the total surface area of all the blocks?
   c The blocks are to be varnished. A tin of varnish covers an area of 4 m². How many tins of varnish are needed to coat each of the 450 blocks once? Show how you worked out your answer.

 Tip

It is useful to draw a rough net of the object to make sure you include all the faces in your surface area calculations.

5 The diagram below shows a metal canister with a plastic lid. Calculate:
   a the volume of the canister, up to the bottom of the lid
   b the surface area of the outside of the metal canister, up to the bottom of the lid
   c the area of the top of the plastic lid.

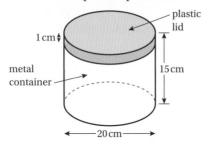

6 The radius of a cylinder is 90 cm. Its height is double its radius. What is its surface area? Give your answer to three significant figures.

7 A rectangular box measures 280 mm × 140 mm × 150 mm. What is the maximum number of smaller cuboids measuring 10 mm × 10 mm × 20 mm that could be packed into the box?

Section 2: Cones and spheres
HOMEWORK 23B

1 Calculate the volume and total surface area of each of the following solids (**a–d**). Give your answers:

   i in terms of π
   ii to three significant figures

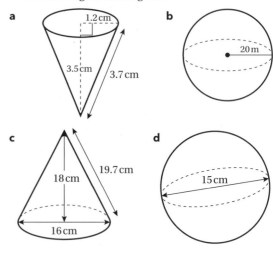

2 Find the height of a cone with a volume of 2500 cm³ and a base of radius 10 cm. Give your answer to three significant figures.

3 Work out the volume of half a sphere of radius 6 cm. Give your answer to three significant figures.

4 A spherical ball has a surface area of 500 cm². What is the diameter of the ball?

HOMEWORK 23C

1 A metal ball is placed in a cylinder of water as shown below. The height of the water rises to 30 cm once the ball is placed in the cylinder. Work out the volume of the water. Give your answer to three significant figures.

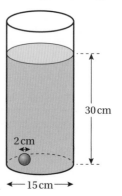

2 A space exploration company made the rocket shown below by combining a cone and a cylinder.

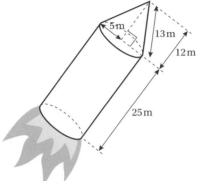

a Work out the exterior surface area of the rocket (including the base).
b Work out the volume of the rocket.
Give your answers to three significant figures.

3 Calculate the volume of metal in the component shown below.

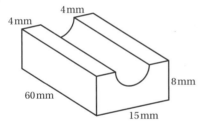

4 Examine the metal breadbin shown on the right and then work out:
a the volume of the breadbin
b its total external area.

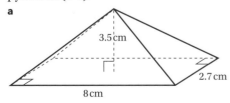

Section 3: Pyramids
HOMEWORK 23D

1 Work out the volume of each of the following pyramids (**a–c**).

a

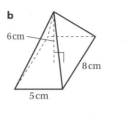

b

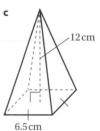

c

2 A rectangular building has a pyramid-shaped roof as shown below. The dimensions of the building are given in metres. Calculate the volume of air inside the building.

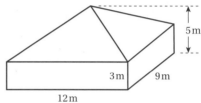

3 A pyramid has a rectangular base of area 27.9 mm². The vertex of the pyramid is 9.3 mm above its base. What is its volume?

4 A triangular-based pyramid is 10.5 m tall. The base is a right-angled triangle with sides adjacent to the right angle measuring 26.6 m and 16.8 m. What is the volume of the pyramid?

5 Sally wants to make a metal pyramid of volume 500 cm³. She starts with a square base 12 cm × 12 cm. How high will her pyramid be?

6 Two hexagonal-based pyramids are glued together base to base. If the area of the base is 3.6 cm² and the length from vertex to apex of the two pyramids is 4.2 cm, what is the volume of the double pyramid shape?

Chapter 23 review

1 Calculate the volume and surface area of each of the solid shapes (**a–f**).

a

b

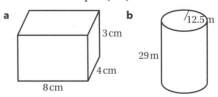

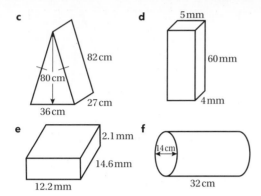

c 82 cm, 80 cm, 27 cm, 36 cm

d 5 mm, 60 mm, 4 mm

e 2.1 mm, 14.6 mm, 12.2 mm

f 14 cm, 32 cm

2 Two solid prisms (A and B) are shown below.

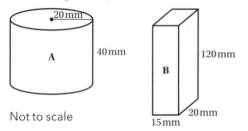

A: 20 mm, 40 mm

B: 120 mm, 20 mm, 15 mm

Not to scale

a Which of the two prisms has the smaller volume? Show how you worked out your answer.

b What is the difference in volume?

c Sketch a net of the cuboid. Your net does not need to be to scale, but you must indicate the dimensions of each face on the net.

d Calculate the surface area of each prism.

3 How many cubes of side 4 cm can be packed into a wooden box measuring 32 cm by 16 cm by 8 cm?

4 **a** Find the volume of a lecture room that is 8 m long, 8 m wide and 3.5 m high.

b Safety regulations state that during an hour-long lecture each person in the room must have 5 m³ of air. Calculate the maximum number of people who can attend an hour-long lecture.

5 A cylindrical tank is 30 m high with an inner radius of 150 cm. Calculate how much water the tank will hold when full. Give your answer to the nearest whole number in:

a m³   **b** litres.

6 A machine shop has four different cuboids of volume 64 000 mm³. Copy and complete the table below and fill in the possible dimensions for each cuboid.

Volume (mm³)	64 000	64 000	64 000	64 000
Length (mm)	80	50		
Breadth (mm)	40		80	
Height (mm)				16

---

24 Further probability

Section 1: Combined events
HOMEWORK 24A

1 Draw a grid to show all possible outcomes when you toss two coins at the same time. Use your diagram to help you answer the following questions.

a What is P(at least one tail)?

b What is P(no tails)?

2 Jess has three green cards numbered 1 to 3 and three yellow cards also numbered 1 to 3.

a Draw up a two-way table to show all possible outcomes when one green card and one yellow card are chosen at random.

b How many possible outcomes are there?

c What is the probability that the number on the cards will be the same? Give your answer as a fraction in its simplest form.

d What is the probability of getting a total < 4 if the scores on the cards are added?

3 Nick and Bev use the two spinners shown below to work out how many moves they can make in a game. They add the scores on the spinners to get the number of moves.

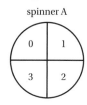
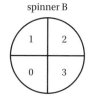

spinner A   spinner B

a Draw up a two-way table to show all the possible pairs of numbers they can get.

b Are all these pairs equally likely? Give a reason for your answer.

c Calculate all the possible numbers of moves they can get by adding the scores.

d Are all numbers of moves equally likely? Give a reason for your answer.

e What number of moves is most likely?

f What is the probability of this number of moves coming up at any turn?

g What is the probability that a player will move:
  i   6 places?   ii   3 places?

HOMEWORK 24B

1 In a group of 12 teenagers, seven had a smartphone, and eight had a tablet. Two students had neither a smartphone nor a tablet. Draw a Venn diagram to represent the data and state how many students had both a smartphone and a tablet.

2 A group of 24 tourists to London were asked which three attractions they had been to. The attractions were the Science Museum, London Eye and Madame Tussauds. One person had been to all three places. Three people had visited the London Eye and Madame Tussauds but not the Science Museum. Two people had visited the Science Museum and Madame Tussauds but not the London Eye. Four people in total had been to the London Eye and 16 people in total had been to the Science Museum. Three of the tourists had been to none of these places.

a Copy and complete the following Venn diagram to show the information above.

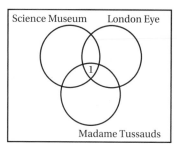

b How many of the tourists went to the Science Museum only?

c How many people only went to the London Eye?

d How many of the tourists visited Madame Tussauds?

e Is it correct to say that 1 in 8 tourists visited none of these places? Give a reason for your answer.

HOMEWORK 24C

1 Draw a tree diagram to show all the ways in which the three letters T O P can be arranged using each letter once only.

2 A new car comes in three colours: red, white and black. The upholstery can be leather or fabric and there is a choice between a two-door or a four-door model. Draw a tree diagram to show all the possible options for choosing a new car.

3 Maire has a bag with a blue counter, red counter and two green counters in it. She also has a card with X on one side and Y on the other. She draws a counter at random and flips the card to land on a letter.

a Draw a tree diagram to show all possible outcomes.

b What is the probability of a green counter and the letter X?

c What is the probability of a red counter and the letter Y?

Section 2: Theoretical probability of combined events

HOMEWORK 24D

1 A blue six-sided dice and a red six-sided dice are rolled together and the scores are added to get a total.

a Draw up a grid to show all possible scores.

b Work out the probability of:
- **i** a total of 12
- **ii** a total of 9
- **iii** a total of at least 10
- **iv** the score is formed by a double
- **v** you get a double and a score of at least 8.

2 A bag contains four green counters, two black counters and a yellow counter. A counter is drawn, replaced and then another is drawn. What is the probability that:
- **a** both counters are yellow?
- **b** both counters are green?
- **c** the first counter is green and the second is black?
- **d** the counters are yellow and green in any order?

3 Josh has a six-sided dice with the faces painted so that three are white, two are red and one is black. He rolls the dice and flips an unbiased coin.
- **a** Draw a probability space diagram to show the possible outcomes.
- **b** Work out the following.
  - **i** P(red, head)
  - **ii** P(white, tail)
  - **iii** P(black, head)

HOMEWORK 24E

1 A bag contains three red counters, four green counters, two yellow counters and one white counter. Two counters are drawn from the bag one after the other, without being replaced.
- **a** Calculate:
  - **i** P(2 red counters)
  - **ii** P(2 green counters)
  - **iii** P(2 yellow counters)
  - **iv** P(white *and then* red).
- **b** What is the probability of drawing a white or yellow counter first and then any colour second?

2 Maria has a bag containing 18 fruit drop sweets. 10 are apple flavoured and 8 are blackberry flavoured. She chooses a sweet at random and eats it. Then she chooses another sweet at random.
- **a** Calculate the probability that:
  - **i** both sweets were apple flavoured
  - **ii** both sweets were blackberry flavoured

- **iii** the first was apple and the second was blackberry
- **iv** the first was blackberry and the second was apple.
- **b** Your answers to **i**, **ii**, **iii** and **iv** should add up to 1. Give a reason why this is the case.

Chapter 24 review

1 There are four red counters and three white counters in a bag. A counter is drawn at random and then replaced. Then a second counter is drawn.
- **a** Draw a tree diagram to represent the possible outcomes.
- **b** Work out:
  - **i** P(*both* counters are red)
  - **ii** P(*both* counters are white)
  - **iii** P(one counter is white *and the other* is red).

2 Two students are to be chosen for a debating team from Amy, James, Nanna, Kenny and Tamara. The teacher choses the team by drawing two names from a hat.
- **a** How many possible outcomes are there?
- **b** What is the probability that:
  - **i** two girls will be chosen?
  - **ii** two boys will be chosen?
  - **iii** James will be on the team?
  - **iv** the team will have one boy and one girl?

3 An octagonal dice is numbered from 1 to 8.
- **a** Draw a tree diagram to show the probability of getting a multiple of 3 (3m) on two successive rolls of the dice.
- **b** Use your tree diagram to work out:
  - **i** P(3m, 3m)
  - **ii** P(*not* 3m, *not* 3m)
  - **iii** P(3m, *not* 3m).

4 Mrs Khan has a choice of ten mobile phone packages. Six of the packages offer free data bundles, five offer a free hands-free kit and three offer both.
- **a** Draw a Venn diagram to show the given information.
- **b** Work out:
  - **i** P(getting free data only)
  - **ii** P(getting free data and a free hands-free kit)
  - **iii** P(getting free data or a hands-free kit).

25 Inequalities

Section 1: Expressing inequalities
HOMEWORK 25A

1 Write each of the following statements as an inequality. List three values that satisfy each inequality.
  a f is less than or equal to 4.
  b x is more than 8 but less than 12.
  c y is greater than 2 but less than 8.
  d x is less than or equal to 12 but greater than 8.
  e x is greater than 4 but less than or equal to 9.

2 Write down three possible solutions for each of these inequalities. Give a value for x and y in each case.
  a $x + y > 2$ b $x + y < 0$ c $x - y > 3$
  d $x - y > 1$ e $xy \leqslant 6$ f $\dfrac{x}{y} \geqslant 4$

Section 2: Number lines
HOMEWORK 25B

1 Draw a number line to represent each inequality.
  a $x > -2$ b $x < -3$
  c $x \leqslant \dfrac{1}{2}$ d $x \geqslant 3$
  e $-1 < x < 3$ f $2 \leqslant x \leqslant 5$
  g $-3 \leqslant x < 0$ h $-3 < x < 4$
  i $-2 < x \leqslant 4$ j $-1 \leqslant x < 2$

2 Write an inequality in terms of x for each number line (**a–l**) as shown.

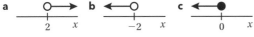

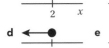
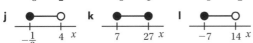

Section 3: Solving inequalities
HOMEWORK 25C

1 Solve these inequalities.
  a $x - 5 \leqslant 3$ b $x + 5 \geqslant -4$ c $\dfrac{1}{2}x \geqslant 5$
  d $-5 + 2x \geqslant 9$ e $5x - 2 \geqslant 1$ f $3x + 6 < 9$

2 Solve for x.
  a $3x \leqslant -9$ b $2 - 4x > 1$ c $\dfrac{3x}{-4} \geqslant -6$
  d $3 - 6x < -8$ e $\dfrac{-x}{4} < 8$ f $\dfrac{-7x}{6} < -7$

3 Solve each inequality. Show your solution on a number line.
  a $1 - 2x > x - 2$ b $2(1 - x) < 5$
  c $3(4 - x) > 12$ d $3x - 5 < x + 6$
  e $4 < 2(2x - 3)$ f $\dfrac{2x - 1}{3} \leqslant 6$

Section 4: Working with inequalities
HOMEWORK 25D

1 Solve each inequality. Show the solution on a number line.
  a $\dfrac{4x}{9} > 8$ b $2x + 7 < -13$
  c $2x - 17 \geqslant 15$ d $2(x + 5) > -8$
  e $4 - \dfrac{x}{4} \leqslant 7$ f $3(x - 2) \leqslant -9$

2 For each of the following, write an inequality to represent the situation and then solve it.
  a A number multiplied by 5 to get a result of less than 5.
  b A number is doubled and then 7 is added to it to get a result less than 19.
  c A number is doubled and then 5 is subtracted from it to get a result of less than 21.

3 Louise is x years old. Her sister Jayne is four years younger. The sum of their ages is less than 28. What are the possible ages that they could be?

4 This is the plan of an L-shaped exhibition space which must be at least 30 m² in area. What lengths must the sides marked x and $2x$ be to meet these conditions?

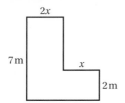

Chapter 25 review

1 Write an inequality to match each number line (**a–c**) shown below.

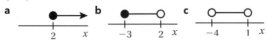

2 Draw number lines to show the following.
  a $x < 0$
  b $2 < x < 6$
  c $-3 < x \leqslant 3$
  d $2(1 - 2x) \leqslant 6$

3 Solve for x.
  a $4x + 3 < 18$
  b $10 + 3x \leqslant 9$
  c $3(x + 2) > 12$
  d $2(5x - 4) \geqslant 20$

4 The sum of two people's ages is no greater than 36. There is 10 years difference between their ages. What possible values could their ages take?

5 Two sportsmen have, between them, played at least 44 games this season. One player is known to have played in 12 more games than the other. What is the least number of games each player could have played?

26 Ratio

Section 1: Introducing ratios
HOMEWORK 26A

1 Express the following as ratios in their simplest form.
  a $120 : 150$
  b $2\frac{3}{4} : 3\frac{2}{3}$
  c 600 g to 3 kilograms
  d 50 mm to 1 metre
  e 12.5 g to 50 g
  f 3 cm to 25 mm
  g 200 ml to 3 l

2 Find the value of x in each of the following.
  a $2 : 3 = 6 : x$
  b $2 : 5 = x : 10$
  c $10 : 15 = x : 6$
  d $\frac{2}{7} = \frac{x}{4}$
  e $\frac{5}{x} = \frac{16}{6}$
  f $\frac{x}{4} = \frac{10}{15}$

3 Write a ratio to compare the salaries of Nisha, Pete and Lara if Nisha earns £40 000 per year, Pete earns £35 000 per year and Lara earns £60 000 per year.

4 A triangle has sides XY = 1.2 cm, XZ = 1.6 cm and YZ = 2.0 cm. Work out the ratio of the sides XY : XZ : YZ in its simplest form.

5 Diego and Raheem are in the same basketball team. In one season Diego scored six more points than Raheem. Write the ratio of the number of points scored by Diego to the number of points scored by Raheem if:
  a Raheem scored 42 points
  b Diego scored 18 points.

6 $\frac{3}{5}$ of the students in a class take French and $\frac{1}{4}$ take Spanish. Find the ratio of those who take French to those who take Spanish.

7 Phone-me-please spends £15 000 on advertising and makes a profit of £120 000. Call-me-quick spends £25 000 on advertising and makes a profit of £200 000. Which company gets the best return on their advertising spend?

 Tip

Think about how you can use ratios to compare the amount spent to the profit made.

8 The ratio of a map or model to the real thing is called the scale factor. If a model of a boat is 40 cm long and the real boat is 16 m long, what is the scale factor?

Section 2: Sharing in a given ratio
HOMEWORK 26B

1 A length of rope 160 cm long must be cut in to two parts so that the lengths are in the ratio 3 : 5. What should the lengths of the parts be?

2 To make salad dressing you mix oil and vinegar in the ratio 2 : 3. Calculate how much oil and how much vinegar you will need to make the following amounts of salad dressing:
   a 50 ml   **b** 600 ml   **c** 750 ml

3 Concrete is made by mixing stone, sand and cement in the ratio 3 : 2 : 1.
   a If 14 wheelbarrows of sand are used, how much stone and cement are needed?
   b How much sand would you need if you were using 18.5 bags of stone?
   c If the concrete contains 3.8 kg of sand, what is the total mass of stone, sand and cement in the mix?

4 The size of three angles of a triangle are in the ratio A : B : C = 2 : 1 : 3. What is the size of each angle?

5 A metal disk consists of three parts silver and two parts copper.
   a If the disk has a mass of 1350 mg, how much silver does it contain?
   b If a disk is found to contain 0.8 grams of silver, how much copper does it contain?

6 In a bag of berry flavoured sweets the ratio of black sweets to red sweets is 3 : 4. If there are 147 sweets in the bag, how many of them are black?

Section 3: Comparing ratios
HOMEWORK 26C

1 Write these ratios in the form of 1 : n.
   a 4 : 9   **b** 400 m : 1.3 km
   c 50 minutes : $1\frac{1}{2}$ hours

2 Write these ratios in the form of n : 1.
   a 12 : 8   **b** 2 m : 40 cm   **c** 2.5 g to 500 mg

3 The ratio of cups of flour to number of cupcakes for two different recipes is A 1 : 13 and B $2\frac{1}{2}$: 32.
   a Which recipe uses the least flour per cupcake?
   b For ratio B, work out how many complete cupcakes can be made with one cup of flour.

4 Amira mixes a drink in the ratio concentrate : water = 1 : 3. Jayne mixes her drink in the ratio 7 : 20. Which mixture gives a stronger concentration?

5 Petar's mark in a test is $\frac{53}{80}$. What will his mark be if it is changed to an equivalent mark out of 50?

6 The ratio of miles to kilometres is 1 : 1.6093
   a Draw a graph to show this relationship.
   b What is the ratio of kilometres to miles in the form of 1 : n?

7 A dessert is made by mixing cream and ice cream in the ratio 5 : 2. A finished dessert contains 400 ml of cream. How much ice cream does it contain?

8 A microscopic organism is drawn using a scale of 1 : 0.01. If the organism is 60 mm long on the diagram, what is its real length?

9 Sarah worked three days a week and earned £600 per month. If she changed to working five days per week, what would her new earnings be?

10 Miguel makes a scale drawing to solve a trigonometry problem. 1 cm on his drawing represents 2 m in real life. He wants to show a 10 m long ladder placed 7 m from the foot of a wall.
   a What length will the ladder be in the diagram?
   b How far will it be from the foot of the wall in the diagram?

HOMEWORK 26D

1 In a golden rectangle, the ratio of length to width can be approximated as 1.6 : 1. Using that ratio, which of the rectangles shown below are golden rectangles?
   A 50 mm × 80 mm   B 30 mm × 20 mm
   C 24 mm × 15 mm   D 36 mm × 21 mm
   E 50 mm × 23 mm   F 18 mm × 28 mm

2 For each rectangle in question 1, work out:
   $\frac{(\text{length} + \text{breadth})}{\text{length}}$ What do you notice?

HOMEWORK 26E

1 Fruit concentrate is mixed with water in the ratio of 1 : 3 to make a fruit drink. How much concentrate would you need to make 1.2 litres of fruit drink?

2 The lengths of the sides of a triangle are in the ratio 4 : 5 : 3. Work out the length of each side if the triangle has a perimeter of 5.4 metres.

3 An alloy is a mixture of metals. Most of the gold used in jewellery is an alloy of pure gold and other metals which are added to make the gold harder. Pure gold is 24 carats (ct), so 18 carat gold is an alloy of gold and other metals in the ratio 18 : 6. In other words, $\frac{18}{24}$ pure gold and $\frac{6}{24}$ other metals.

  a A jeweller makes an 18 ct gold alloy using three grams of pure gold. What mass of other metals does she add?

  b An 18 ct gold chain contains four grams of pure gold. How much other metal does it contain?

  c What is the ratio of gold to other metals in 14 ct gold?

  d What is the ratio of gold to other metals in 9 ct gold?

4 An alloy of 9 ct gold contains gold, copper zinc and silver in the ratio 9 : 12.5 : 2.5

  a Express this ratio in its simplest form.

  b How much silver would you need if your alloy contained six grams of pure gold?

  c How much copper zinc would you need to make a 9 ct alloy using three grams of pure gold?

5 Square A and square B have sides of 125 mm and 6 cm respectively. Find the ratio of their areas without working out the area of each square.

Chapter 26 review

1 Express the following as ratios in their simplest form.

  a $3\frac{1}{2} : 4\frac{3}{4}$ **b** 5 ml to 2.5 litres

  c 125 g to 1 kilogram

2 Divide 600 in the ratio:

  a 7 : 3   **b** 7 : 5   **c** 7 : 13   **d** 7 : 7

3 A triangle of perimeter 360 mm has side lengths in the ratio 3 : 5 : 4.

  a Find the lengths of the sides.

  b Is the triangle right angled? Give a reason for your answer.

4 A model of a car is built to a scale of 1 : 50. If the real car is 2.5 m long, what is the length of the model in centimetres?

5 A school computer lab is one and half times larger than a normal classroom. The locked store room in the computer lab is $\frac{1}{3}$ of the size of a normal classroom. Write a ratio in its simplest form to compare the size of the computer lab to the size of the store room.

27 Proportion

Section 1: Direct proportion

HOMEWORK 27A

1 Which of these could be examples of direct proportion?

  a The time it takes to cover different distances at the same speed

  b The heights of objects and the lengths of their shadows

  c The amount of petrol used to travel different distances

  d The number of chickens you could feed with 20 kg of feed

  e The height of a tree and the number of years since it was planted

  f The area of the sector of a circle and the angle at the centre

2 Work out whether A and B are directly proportional in each case (**a–c**) below.

a

A	2	4	6
B	300	600	900

b

A	1	5	8
B	2	10	15

c

A	1	2	3	4
B	0.1	0.2	0.3	0.4

3 A DVD set costs £25.
   a What is the price of seven DVD sets?
   b What is the price of ten DVD sets?

4 Find the cost of five identically priced items if seven items cost £17.50.

5 If a 3.5 m tall pole casts a 10.5 m shadow, find the length of the shadow cast by a 20 m tall pole at the same time of day.

6 A truck uses 20 litres of diesel to travel 240 kilometres.
   a How much diesel will it use to travel 180 km at the same rate?
   b How far could the truck travel on 45 litres of diesel at the same rate?

HOMEWORK 27B

1 A car travels 30 km in 40 minutes. How long would it take to travel 45 km at the same speed?

2 If a clock gains 20 seconds in four days, how much does it gain in two weeks?

3 Six identical drums of oil weigh 90 kg in total. What do 11.5 drums weigh?

4 An athlete runs 4.5 kilometres in 15 minutes. How far could he run in 35 minutes at the same speed?

5 To make 12 muffins, you need the following:

240 g flour	48 g sultanas
60 g margarine	74 ml milk
24 g sugar	12 g salt

   a How much of each ingredient would you need to make 16 muffins?
   b Express the amount of flour to margarine in this recipe as a ratio.

6 A vendor sells frozen yoghurt in 250 g and 100 g tubs. It costs £1.75 for 250 g and 80 pence for 100 g. Which is the better buy? Show how you worked out your answer.

Section 2: Algebraic and graphical representations
HOMEWORK 27C

1 The graph below shows the directly proportional relationship between lengths in metres (metric) and lengths in feet (imperial).

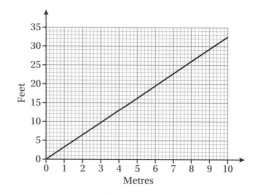

   a Use the graph to estimate how many feet there are in four metres.
   b Given that 1 m = 3.28 feet and one foot = 0.305 m, calculate how many feet there are in four metres.
   c Which is longer:
      i four metres or 12 feet?
      ii 20 feet or 6.5 metres?
   d Mr Bokomo has a length of fabric 9 m long.
      i What is its length to the nearest foot?
      ii He cuts off and sells 1.5 m to Mrs Johannes and 3 feet to Mr Moosa. How much is left in metres?
   e A driveway was 18 feet long. It was resurfaced and extended to be one metre longer than previously. How long is the newly resurfaced driveway in metres?

2 Given that a varies directly with b and that $a = 56$ when $b = 8$,
   a find the value of the constant of proportionality (k)
   b find the value of a when $b = 12$.

Tip

When two quantities are directly proportional then $P = kQ$, where k is a constant.

3 F is directly proportional to m and $F = 16$ when $m = 2$.
  a Find the value of F when $m = 5$.
  b Find the value of m when $F = 36$.

4 y is directly proportional to x^2, and $y = 50$ when $x = 5$.
  a Write the equation for this relationship.
  b Find y if $x = 25$.   **c** Find x if $y = 162$.

Section 3: Inverse proportion
HOMEWORK 27D

1 It takes one employee ten days to complete a project. If another employee joins him, it only takes five days. Five employees can complete the job in two days.
  a Describe this relationship.
  b How long would it take to complete the project with:
    i four employees?   **ii** 20 employees?

2 After a tsunami, ten people have enough fresh water to last them for six days at a set rate per person.
  a How long would the water last, if there were only five people drinking it at the same rate?
  b Two people join the initial group of 10. How long will the water last if it is used at the same rate?

3 A plane travelling at an average speed of 1000 km/h takes 12 hours to complete a journey. How fast would it need to travel to cover the same distance in ten hours?

4 Sanjay has a 50 m long piece of rope. How many pieces can he cut it into if the length of each piece is:
  a 50 cm?   **b** 200 cm?   **c** 625 cm?
  d He cuts the rope into 20 equal lengths. What is the length of each piece?

5 A journey takes three hours when you travel at 60 km/h. How long would the same journey take at a speed of 50 km/h?

6 For each of the following, y is inversely proportional to x. Write an equation expressing y in terms of x if:
  a $y = 0.225$ when $x = 20$
  b $y = 12.5$ when $x = 5$
  c $y = 5$ when $x = 0.4$
  d $y = 0.4$ when $x = 0.7$
  e $y = 0.6$ when $x = 8$

Chapter 27 review

1 A car travels at an average speed of 85 km/h.
  a What distance will the car travel in:
    i 1 hour?   **ii** $4\frac{1}{2}$ hours?   **iii** 15 minutes?
  b How long will it take the car to travel:
    i 30 km?   **ii** 400 km?   **iii** 100 km?

2 A car used 45 litres of fuel to travel 495 km.
  a How far could the car travel on 50 litres of fuel at the same rate?
  b How much fuel would the car use to travel 190 km at the same rate?

3 A hurricane disaster centre has a certain amount of clean water. The length of time the water will last depends on the number of people who come to the centre. Copy the table below and calculate the missing values.

No. of people	120	150	200	300	400
Days the water will last	40	32			

4 It takes six people 12 days to paint a building. Work out how long it would take at the same rate using:
  a 9 people   **b** 36 people.

5 Study the graph below and answer the questions that follow.
  a What does the graph above show?
  b Convert to litres:
    i 10 gallons
    ii 25 gallons
  c Convert to gallons:
    i 15 litres
    ii 120 litres

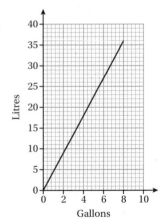

d Naresh says he gets 30 mpg in the city and 42 mpg on the highway in his car.
 i Given that 8 km = 5 miles, convert each rate to km per gallon.
 ii One gallon = 4.546 litres. Convert both rates to kilometres per litre.

28 Graphs of linear functions

Section 1: Plotting graphs

HOMEWORK 28A

1 Draw up a table of values for each equation below. Use −1, 0, 1, 2 and 3 as values of x. In question (**g**) use these values for y.

a $y = x + 3$ **b** $y = 3$ **c** $y = \dfrac{1}{2}x - 1$

d $y = -\dfrac{1}{2}x$ **e** $y = x - 1$ **f** $2x - y = 4$

g $x = 7$ **h** $x + y = -1$

2 Use the values from your tables from question 1 to plot the graphs. Plot graphs (**a–d**) on one set of axes and graphs (**e–h**) on another.

Section 2: Gradient and intercepts of straight-line graphs

HOMEWORK 28B

1 Find the gradient of each line (**a–h**) in the following diagrams.

a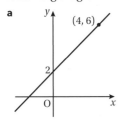

b

c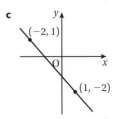

d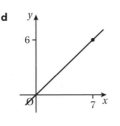

e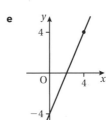

f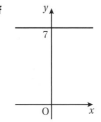

g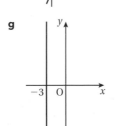

h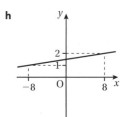

2 Work out the gradient of each of the following graphs (without drawing the graph).

a $y = x$ **b** $y = \dfrac{x}{2} + \dfrac{1}{4}$ **c** $y = \dfrac{4x}{5} - 2$

d $y = 7$ **e** $y = -3x$ **f** $x + 3y = 14$

g $x + y + 4 = 0$ **h** $2x = 5 - y$ **i** $x + \dfrac{y}{2} = -10$

3 For each pair of points, work out the gradient of a line which passes through them.
 a $(0, 0)$ and $(-3, 3)$
 b $(4, 2)$ and $(8, 4)$
 c $(2, -3)$ and $(4, -1)$

4 **a** Draw a set of axes and plot the vertices of quadrilateral ABCD with A = $(0, 3)$, B = $(4, 5)$, C = $(2, 1)$ and D = $(-2, -1)$. Draw in the sides of the quadrilateral.
 b Work out the gradient of each side of the quadrilateral.
 c What is the gradient of diagonal AC?

75

HOMEWORK 28C

1 Write the equation of each graph (**a–e**) shown below.

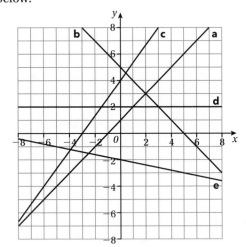

2 Use the gradient and the *y*-intercept to sketch these graphs.
 a $y = 2x + 1$
 b $y = -3x + 2$
 c $y = \frac{1}{2}x + 1$
 d $x - 4y = 2$

3 Work out the *x*- and *y*-intercepts of each line and sketch the graphs.
 a $x + y = 4$
 b $x + 2y = 6$
 c $2x - y = 4$
 d $3x + 2y = 2$

HOMEWORK 28D

1 Does point $(1, 2)$ lie on the line $2x + y = 4$? Show how you worked out your answer.

2 Given that $y = mx + c$, what is the equation of a line with gradient 2 passing through point $(-1, -5)$?

3 The lines $y = x + c$ and $y = 3x + c$ are drawn on the same set of axes. Both lines pass through the point $(3, 7)$. Work out the *y*-intercept (c) of each line.

4 What is the equation of the line that:
 a intersects the *y*-axis at 3 and has a gradient of $-\frac{1}{3}$?

b passes through point $(-8, 15)$ and cuts the *y*-axis at -9?
 c has a gradient of 2 and passes through point $(2, 5)$?
 d passes through $(-4, 0)$ and $(0, 5)$?
 e passes through the origin and point $(-10, 1)$?

Section 3: Parallel lines
HOMEWORK 28E

1 Are the following pairs of lines parallel or not?
 a $y = -3x$ and $y = -3x + 7$
 b $y = 0.8x - 7$ and $y = 8x + 2$
 c $2y = -3x + 2$ and $y = \frac{3}{2}x + 2$
 d $2y - 3x = 2$ and $y = -1.5x + 2$
 e $y = 8$ and $y = -9$
 f $x = -3$ and $x = \frac{1}{2}$

2 What is the equation of a line parallel to $y = x + 5$ and passing through point $(0, -2)$?

3 For lines (A–E) shown in the diagram below:
 a work out the equation of the line
 b work out the equation of a line parallel to each line and passing through point $(0, -7)$.

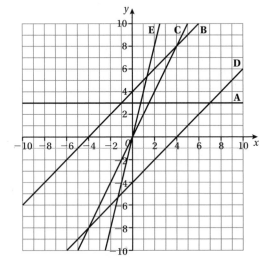

4 If $y = ax - 8$ is parallel to $y = 7x + \frac{5}{2}$, what is the value of a?

5 If $y = bx - 1$ is parallel to $4y - 5x = 7$, what is the value of b?

Section 4: Working with straight-line graphs

HOMEWORK 28F

1. Write down the gradient and the coordinates of the y-intercept of each of the following lines.

   a $y = 3x - 2$ **b** $y = 4x - 2$

   c $y = -x - \dfrac{1}{4}$ **d** $y = \dfrac{3}{4}x + 1$

2. Sketch each of the graphs from question 1 (above), labelling the key features.

3. Find the equation of the line that is:
   a parallel to the line with equation $y = 4x + 1$, but passes through the point $(3, 16)$
   b parallel to the line with equation $y = -3x + 5$, but passes through the point $(7, -8)$
   c parallel to the line with equation $y = 0.5x + 0.3$, but passes through the point $(3, 2.4)$
   d parallel to the line with equation $3x + 4y = 12$, but passes through the point $(2, -1)$
   e parallel to the line with equation $5x - 2y = 18$, but passes through the point $(-3, -4)$.

4. The point $(5, a)$ lies on the line $y = \dfrac{1}{2}x - 1$. What is the value of a?

5. If the point $(b, 7)$ lies on the line $y = 2x + 3$, what is b?

6. If the graph $y = 2x + 6$ passes through points $(3, m)$ and $(n, 2)$, work out the value of m and n.

7. **a** Find the equation of each line (**i–iv**) in the diagrams below.
   b What are the coordinates of points P, Q and R?
   c What is the equation of the line parallel to graph **iii** which passes through the origin?

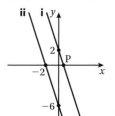
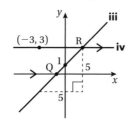

Chapter 28 review

1. Draw up a table of values for $x = -1, 0, 1, 2$ for each equation and use the tables to plot the graphs.

   a $y = \dfrac{1}{2}x$ **b** $y = -\dfrac{1}{2}x + 3$

   c $y = 2$ **d** $y - 2x - 4 = 0$

2. Work out the gradient and the y-intercept of each graph.

   a $y = -2x - 1$ **b** $y + 6 = x$

   c $x - y = 8$ **d** $y = -\dfrac{1}{2}$

   e $2x + 3y = 6$ **f** $y = -x$

3. Work out the equation for each of these lines.
   a A line parallel to $y = -\dfrac{4}{5}x$ which passes through the point $(0, -3)$
   b A line parallel to $2y + 4x = 20$ with a y-intercept of -3
   c A line parallel to $x + y = 5$ which passes through $(1, 1)$
   d A line parallel to the x-axis which passes through $(1, 2)$
   e A line parallel to the y-axis which passes through $(-4, -5)$

4. Work out the gradient of each of the lines (A–H) shown below.

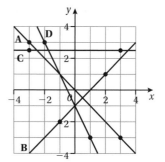
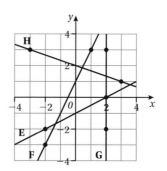

5 What is the equation of each line (**a**–**f**) shown here?

a
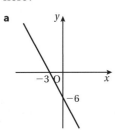

b
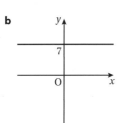

c   **d**   **e**   **f**
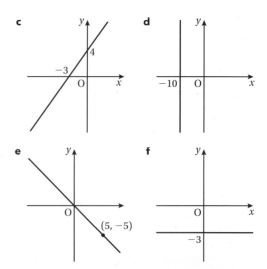

29 Interpreting graphs

Section 1: Graphs of real-world contexts

HOMEWORK 29A

1 The graph below shows the height of a ball when it is thrown in the air.

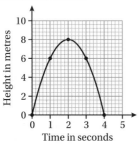

a What is the greatest height the ball reaches?
b How long did it take for the ball to reach this height?
c How high did the ball go in the first second?
d For how long was the ball in the air?
e Estimate for how long the ball was higher than 3 m above the ground.

2 Dabilo and Pam live 200 km apart from each other. They decide to meet up at a shopping centre between their homes one Saturday. Pam travels by bus and Dabilo catches a train. The graph shows both journeys.

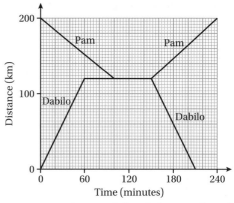

a How much time did Dabilo spend on the train?
b How much time did Pam spend on the bus?
c At what speed did the train travel for the first hour?
d How far was the shopping centre from:
  i Dabilo's home?   **ii** Pam's home?
e What was the average speed of the bus from Pam's home to the shopping centre?
f How long did Dabilo have to wait before Pam arrived?
g How long did the two girls spend together?
h How much faster was Pam's journey on the way home?
i If they left home at 8:00 am, what time did each girl return home after the day's outing?

3 The population of bedbugs in New York City is found to have increased rapidly over a period of four months. The increases in number are given in the table.

Time (months)	0	1	2	3	4
Bedbug population (estimated)	1000	2000	4000	8000	16 000

  a Plot a graph to show the increase over time.
  b When did the number of bedbugs reach 10 000?
  c Estimate the number of bedbugs there will be after six months if the population continues to grow at this rate.

Section 2: Gradients
HOMEWORK 29B

1 The graph shows the concentration of lactic acid in a runner's muscles before, during and after strenuous exercise.

  a What is the normal amount of lactic acid in muscles (based on the graph)?
  b What happens to the level of lactic acid after ten minutes? How can you tell this?
  c The runner stops exerting herself after 10 minutes. What happens to the level of lactic acid after this?
  d How long does it take the level to return to normal?

Lactic acid concentration before, during and after exercise

2 The following graph represents a cyclist's journey from home to the post office. Match each label below to a labelled section (A–F) on the graph.

Stopped   Constant speed   Slowing down

Quick decrease in speed to a stop

Slowed to a stop   Quick increase in speed

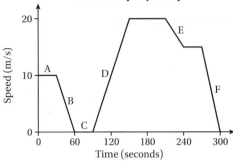

Sarah's bicycle journey

3 The graph below shows what percentage of her salary Annabel spends paying bills.

  a What time period is represented on the graph?
  b What percentage of Annabel's salary is used to pay bills in February?
  c At what point does she have no bills to pay?
  d When do her bill payments increase sharply? What might have caused this?
  e One month Annabel uses almost $\frac{3}{4}$ of her salary to repay a loan. When was this?
  f Write a short description of Annabel's financial situation over the time period.

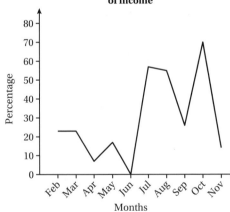

Monthly payments as a percentage of income

Chapter 29 review

1 The following distance–time graph shows a cyclist's journey during a cross-country cycle ride.

  a Calculate the cyclist's average speed for:
    i the first ten minutes of the ride
    ii the whole ride.
  b How far was the cyclist from the start/finish point after two hours?

c The cyclist took 45 minutes to fix a problem with her brakes. How far was the cyclist from the starting point when she got the puncture?

Distance–time graph of a cyclist's journey

Distance from start (km) vs *Time (minutes)*

2 The following graph shows the speed, in metres per second, of a car as it comes to rest from a speed of 10 m/s.

a Calculate the rate at which the car is slowing down during the first three seconds.

b Calculate the distance travelled during the ten-second period shown on the graph.

c Calculate the average speed of the car for this ten-second period.

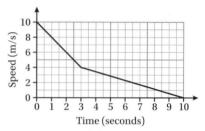

Speed (m/s) vs *Time (seconds)*

30 Vector geometry

Section 1: Vector notation and representation

HOMEWORK 30A

1 The diagram below shows eight vectors. Use vector notation (as shown for the first vector below) to write down each of the others.

$$\overrightarrow{AB} = \begin{pmatrix} 3 \\ 1 \end{pmatrix}$$

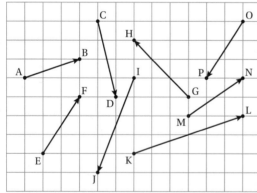

> **Tip**
>
> In vectors the horizontal direction is given by the top figure, the vertical direction is given by the bottom figure.

2 Draw a pair of axes where x and y range from -6 to $+10$. Plot the point A (1, 2). Plot the points B, C, D, E, F and G where:

$$\overrightarrow{AB} = \begin{pmatrix} 4 \\ -2 \end{pmatrix} \quad \overrightarrow{AC} = \begin{pmatrix} 3 \\ 7 \end{pmatrix} \quad \overrightarrow{AD} = \begin{pmatrix} -4 \\ -3 \end{pmatrix}$$

$$\overrightarrow{AE} = \begin{pmatrix} 7 \\ -4 \end{pmatrix} \quad \overrightarrow{AF} = \begin{pmatrix} 9 \\ 6 \end{pmatrix} \quad \overrightarrow{AG} = \begin{pmatrix} -7 \\ -5 \end{pmatrix}$$

3 **a** Find the vector from point P with coordinates (2, 6) to the point Q with coordinates (−3, 5).

b What is the vector $\overrightarrow{QP}$?

4 **a** Find the vector from point A with coordinates (−3, 4) to the point B with coordinates (−7, −2).

b Use your answer to find the coordinates of the midpoint of AB.

5 The following vectors describe how to move between points P, Q, R and S.

$$\overrightarrow{PQ} = \begin{pmatrix} -3 \\ 5 \end{pmatrix} \quad \overrightarrow{QR} = \begin{pmatrix} 3 \\ 0 \end{pmatrix} \quad \overrightarrow{RP} = \begin{pmatrix} 0 \\ -5 \end{pmatrix} \quad \overrightarrow{QS} = \begin{pmatrix} 6 \\ -5 \end{pmatrix}$$

a Draw a diagram to show how the points are positioned to form the quadrilateral PQRS.

b What shape is PQRS?

6 The vector $\begin{pmatrix} 9 \\ -7 \end{pmatrix}$ describes the displacement from point A to point B.

a What is the vector from point B to point A?

b Point A has coordinates $(-4, 3)$. What are the coordinates of point B?

Section 2: Vector arithmetic
HOMEWORK 30B

1 $\mathbf{p} = \begin{pmatrix} -3 \\ 4 \end{pmatrix}$ $\mathbf{q} = \begin{pmatrix} 3 \\ -2 \end{pmatrix}$ $\mathbf{r} = \begin{pmatrix} 7 \\ -3 \end{pmatrix}$ $\mathbf{s} = \begin{pmatrix} -9 \\ -7 \end{pmatrix}$

Write each of these as a single vector.

a $\mathbf{p} + \mathbf{q}$ **b** $\mathbf{q} - \mathbf{r}$

c $\mathbf{s} - \mathbf{r}$ **d** $\mathbf{q} + \mathbf{s}$

e $3\mathbf{p}$ **f** $-4\mathbf{r}$

g $\mathbf{p} + \mathbf{q} + \mathbf{r}$ **h** $3\mathbf{q} - \mathbf{r}$

i $2\mathbf{r} + 3\mathbf{s}$ **j** $2\mathbf{p} + 3\mathbf{r} - \mathbf{s}$

2 Write down three vectors which are parallel to $\begin{pmatrix} -2 \\ 4 \end{pmatrix}$.

3 Find the values of x, y and z in these vector calculations.

a $\begin{pmatrix} x \\ -3 \end{pmatrix} + \begin{pmatrix} 3 \\ -7 \end{pmatrix} = \begin{pmatrix} -1 \\ y \end{pmatrix}$ **b** $\begin{pmatrix} 6 \\ x \end{pmatrix} - \begin{pmatrix} y \\ -2 \end{pmatrix} = \begin{pmatrix} 8 \\ -5 \end{pmatrix}$

c $\begin{pmatrix} x \\ -5 \end{pmatrix} + \begin{pmatrix} 5 \\ y \end{pmatrix} = \begin{pmatrix} 0 \\ 0 \end{pmatrix}$ **d** $\begin{pmatrix} 4 \\ -2 \end{pmatrix} = x\begin{pmatrix} 12 \\ -6 \end{pmatrix}$

e $x\begin{pmatrix} -4 \\ -3 \end{pmatrix} + y\begin{pmatrix} 2 \\ 3 \end{pmatrix} = \begin{pmatrix} -16 \\ -15 \end{pmatrix}$

4 In the diagram below $\overrightarrow{AB} = \begin{pmatrix} 18 \\ 12 \end{pmatrix}$.

The ratio of AC : CB is $1 : 2$

a Find $\overrightarrow{AC}$

b Find $\overrightarrow{CB}$

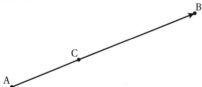

5 These vectors describe how to move between the points P, Q, R and S, which are four sides of a quadrilateral.

$\overrightarrow{PQ} = \begin{pmatrix} 4 \\ 1 \end{pmatrix}$ $\overrightarrow{QS} = \begin{pmatrix} -1 \\ -5 \end{pmatrix}$ $\overrightarrow{PR} = \begin{pmatrix} 7 \\ -3 \end{pmatrix}$

a What can you say about sides PQ and SR?

b What type of quadrilateral is PQRS?

6 ABCD is a quadrilateral. If the vectors $\overrightarrow{AD}$ and $\overrightarrow{BC}$ are parallel and of equal length, what shape could ABCD be?

Section 3: Mixed practice
HOMEWORK 30C

1 In the diagram below $\overrightarrow{AB} = \begin{pmatrix} 8 \\ 3 \end{pmatrix}$ and $\overrightarrow{BC} = \begin{pmatrix} 2 \\ -4 \end{pmatrix}$.
M is the midpoint of AB.
Find:

a $\overrightarrow{BA}$ **b** $\overrightarrow{BA} + \overrightarrow{AC}$ **c** $\overrightarrow{AM}$

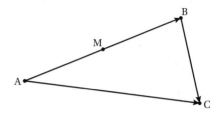

2 Two triangles ABC and DEF have the vertices
$A = (1, 4)$, $B = (5, 3)$, $C = (6, 7)$,
$D = (5, 2)$, $E = (9, 1)$ and $F = (10, 5)$.

a Compare the vectors:

   i $\overrightarrow{AB}$ and $\overrightarrow{DE}$

   ii $\overrightarrow{AC}$ and $\overrightarrow{DF}$

b What must be true of the triangles ABC and DEF?

3 A plane travels 9 km west and 12 km south. What vector has it travelled?

4 The vector from P to Q is $\begin{pmatrix} 8 \\ -5 \end{pmatrix}$ and from Q to R is $\begin{pmatrix} -4 \\ 3 \end{pmatrix}$.

What is the vector from:

a P to R?   **b** Q to P?

c Q to the midpoint of QR?

d R to the midpoint of PQ?

5 The vector from F to G is $\begin{pmatrix} 5 \\ -2 \end{pmatrix}$. The vector from H to I is parallel to $\overrightarrow{FG}$, and I is three times the distance from H as G is from F. What is the vector from H to I?

6 A chessboard is made up of 8×8 squares, giving a total of 64 squares. A knight can move two squares horizontally and one square vertically or two squares vertically and one square horizontally.
Assuming there is nothing in the way, what is the smallest number of moves that a Knight can take to get from one corner square to the opposite diagonal corner square?

Chapter 30 review

1 Write down why (3, 4) is different from $\begin{pmatrix} 3 \\ 4 \end{pmatrix}$.

2 Which of the following vectors are parallel?

A $\begin{pmatrix} 3 \\ 4 \end{pmatrix}$ B $\begin{pmatrix} 8 \\ 9 \end{pmatrix}$ C $\begin{pmatrix} 6 \\ -6 \end{pmatrix}$

D $\begin{pmatrix} 4 \\ 3 \end{pmatrix}$ E $\begin{pmatrix} 9 \\ 12 \end{pmatrix}$ F $\begin{pmatrix} 2 \\ -2 \end{pmatrix}$

3 Calculate:

a $\begin{pmatrix} 4 \\ -5 \end{pmatrix} + \begin{pmatrix} 5 \\ 7 \end{pmatrix}$ **b** $\begin{pmatrix} 6 \\ 3 \end{pmatrix} - \begin{pmatrix} 5 \\ -2 \end{pmatrix}$ **c** $4\begin{pmatrix} 1 \\ -6 \end{pmatrix}$

4 In the diagram below, M is the midpoint of BC. A is the point (1, 1), B is the point (7, 5) and C is the point (5, 7).
Find:

a $\overrightarrow{AC}$ **b** $\overrightarrow{CM}$ **c** $\overrightarrow{AM}$

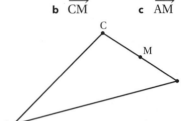

31 Transformations in a plane

Section 1: Reflections
HOMEWORK 31A

1 A child has been making potato prints (**a–b**). The paint is still wet. On squared paper, sketch what will happen for each print if the paper is folded along the dotted line.

a

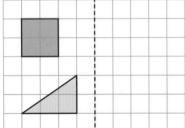

b

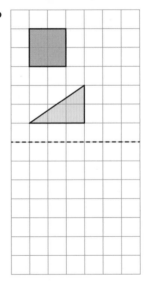

 Tip

Reflections don't change the shape or size of a shape.

 Tip

The image and the reflection are always the same distance away from the mirror line.

2 Copy each of the following grids (**a–c**) and reflect the given shape in the given mirror line.

a

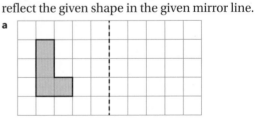

b

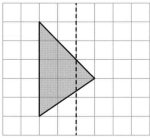

c

2 Copy the grid. Reflect the shape shown in the line $y = x$ and the resultant image in the line $y = -x$.

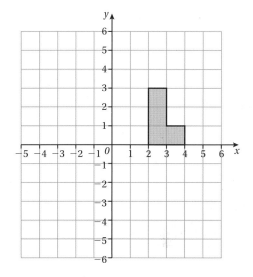

HOMEWORK 31B

1 Copy the grid. Reflect the triangle shown in the line $x = 2$ and the resultant image in the line $y = -2$.

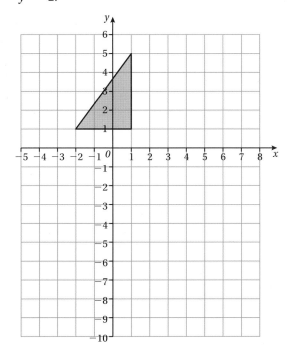

3 Copy the grid. Carry out the seven reflections listed below using the shapes provided in the diagram.

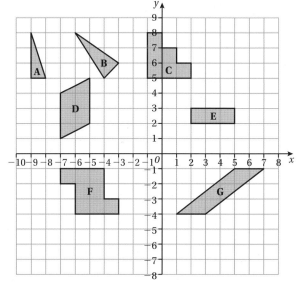

a Shape A in the line $x = -6$
b Shape B in the line $y = 3$
c Shape C in the line $y = x$
d Shape D in the line $x = -5$
e Shape E in the line $y = x$
f Shape F in the line $y = -2$
g Shape G in the line $y = -x$

HOMEWORK 31C

1 Find the equation of the mirror line in each of the following reflections (**a–c**).

a

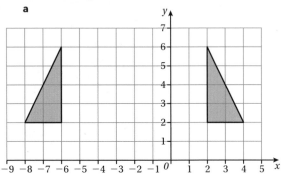

b

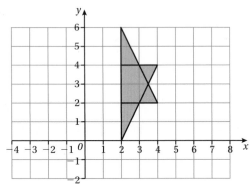

c

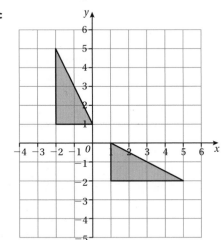

2 Using the following diagram, describe the reflection that takes:

a shape G to D

b shape F to A

c shape C to H

d shape B to C

e shape E to D

f shape A to H.

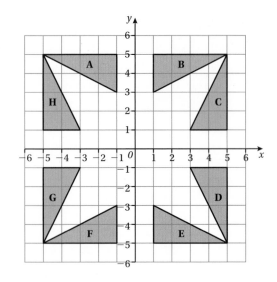

3 Trace each pair of shapes (**a–c**) below and construct the mirror line for each reflection.

a   **b**   **c**

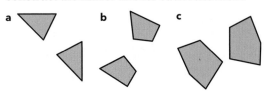

Section 2: Translations

HOMEWORK 31D

1 Copy and translare each shape as directed.

a 4 right and 5 up

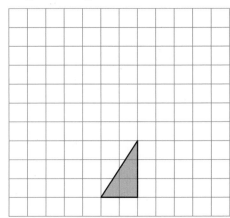

b 4 left and 5 up

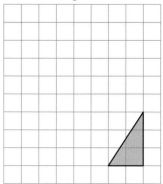

c 2 right and 6 up

Tip

Remember to go across left or right before up or down.

HOMEWORK 31E

1 Copy the diagram and translate the shape using the given vectors (**a–d**).

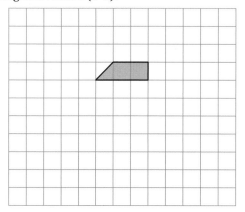

a $\begin{pmatrix} 4 \\ 2 \end{pmatrix}$ **b** $\begin{pmatrix} 3 \\ -2 \end{pmatrix}$ **c** $\begin{pmatrix} -4 \\ -5 \end{pmatrix}$ **d** $\begin{pmatrix} -4 \\ -1 \end{pmatrix}$

2 Copy the diagram and translate each shape by the vector given for it below.

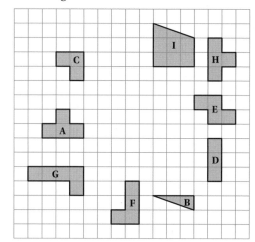

A $\begin{pmatrix} 5 \\ -2 \end{pmatrix}$ B $\begin{pmatrix} -3 \\ 7 \end{pmatrix}$ C $\begin{pmatrix} 7 \\ -5 \end{pmatrix}$

D $\begin{pmatrix} -8 \\ 4 \end{pmatrix}$ E $\begin{pmatrix} -4 \\ -3 \end{pmatrix}$ F $\begin{pmatrix} 3 \\ 7 \end{pmatrix}$

G $\begin{pmatrix} 6 \\ 6 \end{pmatrix}$ H $\begin{pmatrix} -8 \\ -6 \end{pmatrix}$ I $\begin{pmatrix} -3 \\ -5 \end{pmatrix}$

HOMEWORK 31F

1 The hatched square shown in the diagram below has been made by fitting the shaded pieces together as shown. Write down the vector that will translate each shaded piece to the correct part of the corresponding hatched square.

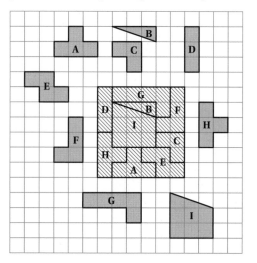

Section 3: Rotations
HOMEWORK 31G

1 Copy and rotate each shape (**a** and **b**) as directed.
   a 90° clockwise about the origin

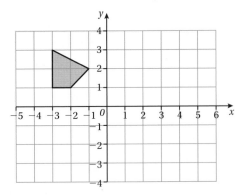

   b 90° anticlockwise about the point (1, 1)

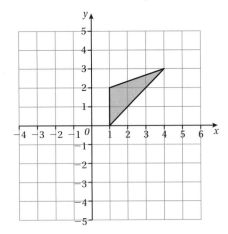

2 Copy and rotate each shape (**a** and **b**) as directed about the marked centre of rotation.
   a 90° clockwise

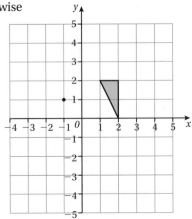

   b 90° anticlockwise

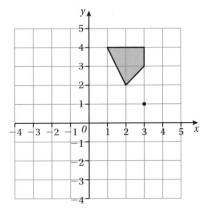

3 Copy and rotate the arrow shape shown 90°, 180° and 270° clockwise about the origin.

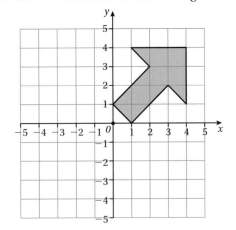

4 Copy and rotate the shape shown 90°, 180° and 270° clockwise about the point (−1, 1).

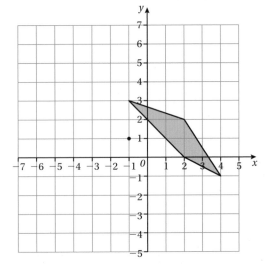

5 Copy and rotate the image shown 120°, and 240° about the point (2, 1).

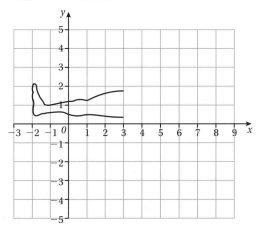

6 The image shown below was designed by drawing a triangle and rotating it around the point (1, 1) in multiples of 90°.
   a Write down the coordinates of each of the marked points.
   b What would be the coordinates if the shape A was rotated in multiples of 90° around the point (2, 2)?

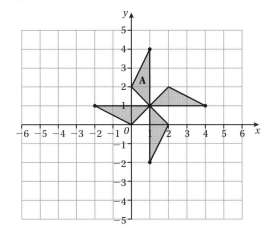

HOMEWORK 31H

1 Describe each of the following rotations (**a–b**) shown below.

a

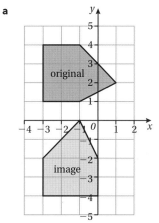

b

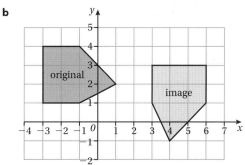

2 The diagram below shows part of a crossword grid. Copy the diagram on squared paper. Label the bottom left corner the origin, and label the axes.
   a Rotate the square formed by (0, 6), (6, 6), (6, 12) and (0, 12) 90°, 180° and 270° about the point (6, 6) and complete the grid.
   b How many white squares are there?

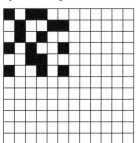

Chapter 31 review

1 Which of the following statements are true? Give reasons, including diagrams if necessary.

a Any reflected object is congruent to its image.

b A reflection about the *x*-axis is the same as a rotation of 180°.

c A triangle ABC such that A is (5, 3), B is (4, 2) and C is (6, 6) is rotated 180° about the origin. The coordinates of the image are A′ = (−5, −6), B′ = (−5, −3), C′ = (−2, −4)

2 The triangle XYZ has vertices X = (6, 3), Y =(3, 2) and Z = (4, 6). Write down the coordinates of the images of X, Y and Z after the following transformations.

a Translation by the vector $\begin{pmatrix} 5 \\ 2 \end{pmatrix}$

b Rotation of 90° clockwise about the point (2, 2)

c Reflection in the line $y = 2$

32 Construction and loci

Section 1: Geometrical instruments
HOMEWORK 32A

1 Use a ruler and protractor to draw and label the following angles.

a ABC = 35°　**b** DEF = 129°　**c** PQR = 100°

> **Tip**
>
> A sharp pencil and a good quality pair of compasses which has been tightened are essential to construct angles properly.

2 Write down how you would use a protractor marked from 0° to 180° to measure a reflex angle.

3 Draw line AB which is 6.2 cm long. At A, measure and draw angle BAC = 45°. At B, measure and draw angle ABD = 98°.

4 Use a pair of compasses to construct:

a a circle of radius 3 cm

b a circle of diameter 10 cm

c two circles, one of diameter 3 cm and another of diameter 4 cm whose circumferences touch once.

5 Follow stops (**a**–**d**) to construct a triangle inside a circle.

a Draw a circle of radius 45 mm and centre O.

b Use a ruler to draw any two radii of the circle.

c Label them OA and OB. Join point A to point B to form triangle AOB.

d Measure the angles AOB, OBA and BAO. What sort of triangle have you constructed?

Section 2: Ruler and compass constructions
HOMEWORK 32B

1 Measure and draw the following line segments. Find the midpoint of each by construction.

a AB = 11 cm　　**b** CD = 36 mm

c EF = 7.5 cm

> **Tip**
>
> Make sure you know how to find a midpoint by construction.

2 Draw an angle of 74°. Bisect the angle without measuring. Check your accuracy by measuring.

3 Draw the following angles and then, using only a ruler and pair of compasses, bisect each angle.

a An angle of 68°

b An angle of 156°

c An angle of 120°

4 Draw a triangle ABC where AB = 6 cm, BC = 7 cm and AC = 8 cm.
  a Construct the bisector of each angle.
  b Use the point where the bisectors meet as the centre and draw a circle whose radius is the shortest distance to the side of the triangle
  c What do you notice about this circle?

5 Draw AB = 90 mm. Insert any point C above AB.
  a Construct CX ⊥ AB.
  b Draw CD // AB.

6 Point C lies above the line AB. What line would represent the shortest distance from C to AB?

Section 3: Loci
HOMEWORK 32C

1 Sketch the point, path or area that each locus will produce.
  a Points that are 50 m from a flagpole at point X.
  b The area of grass a goat can eat if tethered to the corner of a rectangular field where the length of rope is the same length as the short side of the rectangle.
  c Points that are equidistant from both tracks of a single railway line.
  d Points that are 30 m from the centre of a shot-put circle within the measuring sector.

2 Accurately construct the locus of a point 6 cm from a point A.

Tip
· A locus is a set of points that satisfy the same rule.

3 Draw angle ABC = 70°. Accurately construct the locus of points equidistant from AB and BC.

Tip
Remember to leave your construction arcs.

4 Draw PQ 50 mm long. Construct the locus of points 2 cm from PQ.

5 Draw a rectangle ABCD with AB = 7 cm and BC = 5 cm.
  a Shade the locus of points that are closer to AB than CD and within the rectangle.
  b Shade the locus of points that are less than 2 cm from A and within the rectangle.
  c Construct the locus of points that are equidistant from AD and BC and within the rectangle.

Section 4: Applying your skills
HOMEWORK 32D

1 Draw line PQ = 6.4 cm. Construct RS, the perpendicular bisector of PQ.
Draw RS so that it is 6.4 cm long and the midpoint of RS is at the same point as the midpoint of PQ. Construct the locus of points which are 3.2 cm from each of P, Q, R and S.

Tip
These problems involve careful and accurate construction. Make sure you use a ruler and a pair of compasses.

2 Construct a parallelogram with sides of 5.5 cm and 3.2 cm and a longest diagonal of length 7 cm. How long is the other diagonal?

3 Accurately construct a square of side 62 mm.

4 Construct quadrilateral PQRS such that PSR is a right angle, SRQ is a right angle, QR = 2PS and SR = 5 cm. What kind of quadrilateral is this?

5 Two towns C and D lie 6 km apart. Two TV transmitters P and Q lie 5 km apart, equidistant from the line CD. The line PQ is perpendicular to CD 2 km from C. Each transmitter can transmit 3.5 km in any direction.
  a Draw a diagram to show the range of the transmitters.
  b If the range of the transmitters was increased to 4.5 km, would the residents of D be able to receive TV signals?

Chapter 32 review

1 **a** Draw an angle of precisely 68°.
   b Bisect this angle.

2 Draw a line PQ which is 45 mm long. Use this line as the diameter of a circle.

3 Draw a line AB of length 8.4 cm and find its midpoint by construction. Show the locus of points that are equidistant from A and B on your diagram.

4 Town A is due south of Town B and they are 60 km apart. Town C is 55 km from Town A and 45 km from Town B to the east side of both towns.
   a Draw a scale diagram to show the location of Town C in relation to the other two towns. Use a scale of 1 cm : 5 km.
   b A road runs from B such that it is equidistant from both AB and BC. Show the position of the road on your drawing.

c A mobile phone mast is to be placed between the three towns so that a signal can reach all three but using the shortest range possible. Show on your diagram the best position for the mast.

5 A train platform is to be built either side of a straight pair of railway tracks which are 1450 mm apart. Each platform must be 450 mm away from the edge of the track and parallel to it. Construct an accurate scale drawing of a 1 m section of the new platforms.

6 A haulage company has a yard that is rectangular and measures 45 m by 65 m. For security there are cameras that rotate in one pair of opposite corners. The range of the cameras is 50 m.
   a Draw an accurate scale diagram to show whether the entire yard is watched by the security cameras.
   b Is it possible to move the cameras so that the entire yard is watched?

33 Similarity

Section 1: Similar triangles
HOMEWORK 33A

1 There are pairs of similar triangles in the diagrams (a–c). Use the correct terminology to identify the matching angles and the sides that are in proportion.

a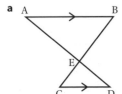

b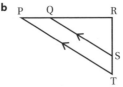

c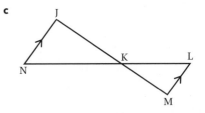

> **Tip**
>
> 'Similar' means exactly the same shape, but a different size. All circles are similar.

2 Are the following pairs of triangles similar? Give a reason for each of your answers.

a

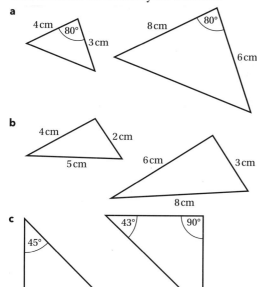

b

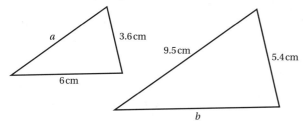

c

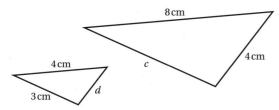

d What is the ratio of the side lengths of the smaller triangle to the side lengths of the larger triangle in part **a** and in part **b** above?

3 **a** The two triangles shown are similar. Find the missing lengths a and b.

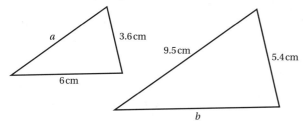

4 The two triangles below are similar. Find the missing lengths c and d.

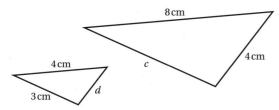

b What is the ratio of the side lengths of the smaller triangle to the side lengths of the larger triangle? Express the ratio using whole numbers in its simplest form.

5 Find the lengths of sides labelled e and f in the similar triangles below.

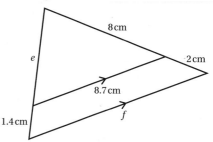

Section 2: Enlargements
HOMEWORK 33B

1 Enlarge each shape shown below as directed.

a Enlarge shape A by a scale factor 2.

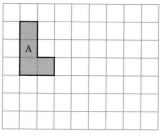

b Enlarge shape B by a scale factor of 1.5

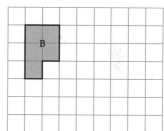

c Enlarge shape C by a scale factor of $\frac{1}{2}$.

> **Tip**
>
> Remember to increase each side by the correct scale factor.

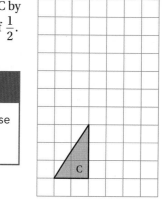

d For each of the enlargements above, what is the ratio of the area of the object to the area of its image after the enlargement?

HOMEWORK 33C

1 Enlarge each shape shown using the scale factor given and the centre of enlargement shown.

Shape a   Scale factor 2

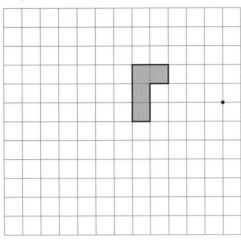

Shape b   Scale factor 1.5

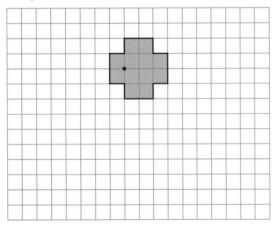

Shape c   Scale factor $\frac{1}{2}$

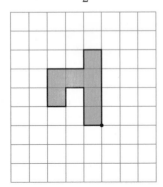

2 Enlarge the triangle below by a scale factor of 1.5, using the origin as the centre of enlargement.

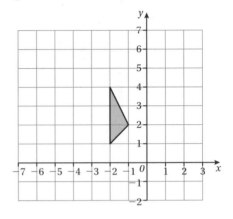

3 Enlarge the shape below by a scale factor of $\frac{1}{2}$ with the centre of enlargement at $(-5, 3)$.

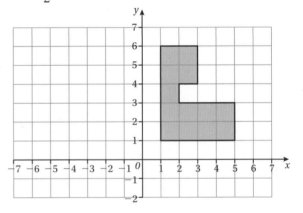

4 Enlarge the shape below by a scale factor of 2 with the centre of enlargement at $(0, 3)$.

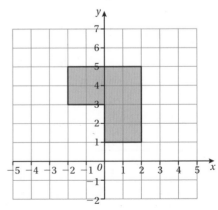

HOMEWORK 33D

1 Which of the following photographs (**a–c**) is an enlargement of the original shown here?

a

b

c

2 Describe each of the following enlargements of the original shape shown in darker shading, giving the scale factor and the centre of enlargement.

a

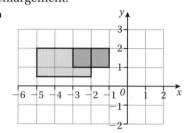

b

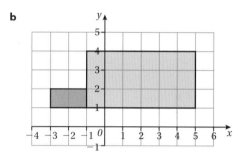

c

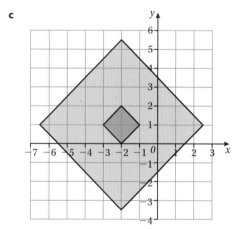

Section 3: Similar polygons
HOMEWORK 33E

1 Decide whether each statement is true or false. Give a reason for each of your answers.
  a All rectangles are similar.
  b All rectangles whose length is twice its width are similar.
  c All regular hexagons are similar.
  d All equilateral triangles are similar.
  e All isosceles triangles are similar.

2 Sketch the following pairs of shapes and decide if they are similar. Give a reason for each of your answers.

    a Rectangle ABCD with AB = 6 cm and BC = 4 cm; Rectangle EFGH with EF = 9 cm and FG = 6 cm

    b Rectangle ABCD with AB = 10 cm and BC = 14 cm; Rectangle EFGH with EF = 7 cm and FG = 11 cm

    c Rectangle ABCD with AB = 12 cm and BC = 9 cm; Rectangle EFGH with EF = 8 cm and FG = 6 cm

3 The shapes shown below are similar. Find the lengths of the sides a and b.

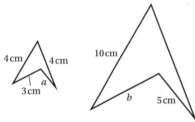

4 In the diagram below the shape PQRS has been created by enlarging ABCD by a scale factor of 2.5. If AB = 2.5 cm, BC = 6 cm, CD = 7 cm and DA = 3.5 cm, find the lengths PQ, QR, RS and SP.

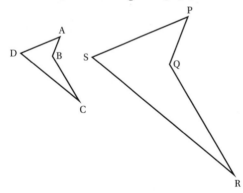

5 On a plan a large square building has side lengths of 15 mm. In reality the building is a 750 metre square.

    a What is the scale factor of the enlargement of the plan (compared to the original building size)?

    b Write this scale as a ratio.

Chapter 33 review

1 **a** Prove that the triangle ABC shown is similar to the triangle ADE.

b Find the lengths AB and BC.

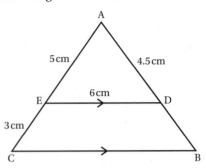

2 A tent manufacturer makes similar shaped tents in three sizes.

A small tent has a width of 1.5 m and a height of 2 m. A medium tent is 1.8 m wide and a large tent is 2.7 m high.

    a How high is a medium tent?

    b How wide is a large tent?

3 Draw an enlargement of the shape shown, scale factor $\frac{1}{2}$ using the centre of enlargement indicated.

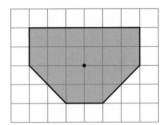

4 Draw an enlargement of this shape, scale factor 1.5 with the centre of enlargement at $(0, 4)$.

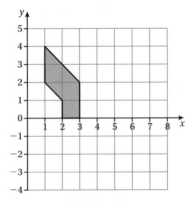

5 Are all parallelograms similar shapes? Give a reason for your answer.

6 Are all kites similar shapes? Give a reason for your answer.

34 Congruence

Section 1: Congruent triangles
HOMEWORK 34A

1 Which of the following pairs of triangles shown below are congruent? Give a reason for each of your answers.

a

b

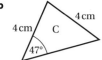

c

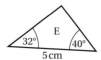 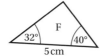

d

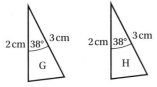

2 **a** Are triangles ABC and DEC shown below congruent?
b Write down how you know.
c What must be true of the point C?

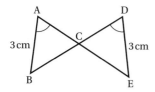

3 Give a reason why triangles FGI and HGI shown below are congruent.

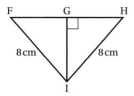

4 AB and DE in the diagram below are parallel. Prove that ABC and EDC are congruent.

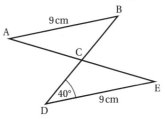

5 ABCD shown below is a rectangle. E is the midpoint of AB. Prove that AED and BEC are congruent.

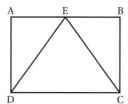

6 The shape ABCDE shown below is a regular pentagon. The point F is the midpoint of CD. Prove that the triangles ABG and AEG are congruent.

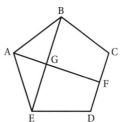

Section 2: Applying congruency
HOMEWORK 34B

1 In the diagram shown below, prove that ABC is congruent to ADC.

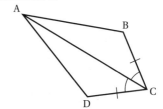

95

2 What shape is PQRS shown below? Give a reason for your answer.

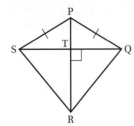

3 **a** In the diagram shown below, what type of triangle is ABD?

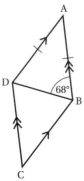

b What is the size of the angle DCB?

c What shape is ABCD?

4 ABCDEF shown below is a regular hexagon.
a Which triangles are congruent?
b What is the size of the angle FAD?
c Which other angle is the same size as FAD?

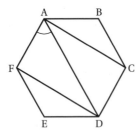

5 In the diagram shown below, ABCD is a parallelogram.
Prove that the angle ADC = ABC.

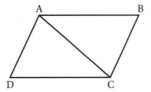

Chapter 34 review

1 Which of the pairs of triangles (**a–c**) in the diagrams below are congruent? Give reasons for your answers.

a

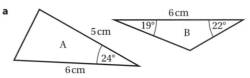

b

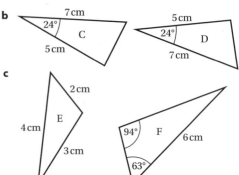

c

2 In the diagram shown below, TP = TQ. PR = QS. The angle TPQ = the angle TQS Prove that the angle QRT = QST.

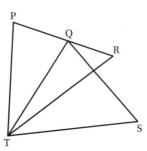

3 The triangle ABC shown below is isosceles, with AB = AC. CE = DB. Prove that the angle ADE = AED.

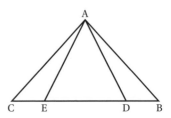

35 Pythagoras' theorem

Section 1: Finding the length of the hypotenuse

HOMEWORK 35A

1 The diagram below shows a right-angled triangle with squares drawn on each side. Write down a sentence describing the relationship between the areas of the squares.

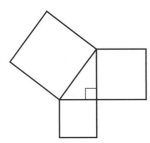

Tip

Pythagoras' theorem only works for right-angled triangles.

HOMEWORK 35B

1 Calculate:
   a 6^2 b 6.2^2
   c 135^2 d 12.6^2
   e $\sqrt{5}$ f $\sqrt{10}$
   g $\sqrt{24}$ h $\sqrt{42}$

2 Find the length of the hypotenuse in each of the following right-angled triangles (**a–c**).
   Give your answers to three significant figures where appropriate.

a
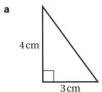

b
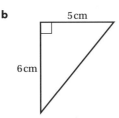

c
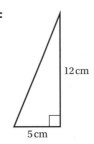

3 Mezut has calculated the hypotenuse of the right-angled triangle shown below to be 18 cm.
   a Write down why you know he is wrong.
   b What is the length of the hypotenuse?

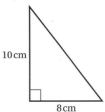

Section 2: Finding the length any side

HOMEWORK 35C

1 Find the length of the unmarked side in each of the right-angled triangles (**a–d**) shown below. Give your answers to three significant figures where appropriate.

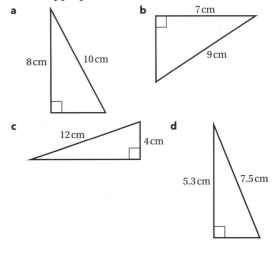

2 The diagram below shows a kite. Use your knowledge of shapes and Pythagoras' theorem to find the missing lengths in the diagram.

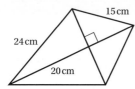

3 The diagram below represents a perpendicular radio mast and two wires which are attached to the top of the mast. If each wire is 45 m long and the mast is 32.6 m high, how far apart are the two wires on the ground?

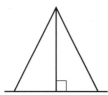

4 A new pyramid is discovered in Egypt, and explorers are able to measure how wide it is at the base and the length of the sloping side , from the top of the pyramid to the mid-point of the base, as shown in the cross section diagram below. How high above the ground is the top of the pyramid?

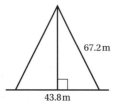

5 A right angled triangle has two sides of length 10 cm and 12 cm. What are the two possible lengths of the other side in this triangle?

6 A sail on a sailing ship is a right angled triangle as shown. If the sail is 5.6 m wide at its base and has a hypotenuse of 11.6 m, how high does it reach up the mast?

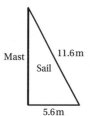

Section 3: Proving whether a triangle is right angled
HOMEWORK 35D

1 The lengths of a number of triangles are given below. In each case, work out which triangles are right angled.
  a 5, 12, 13
  b 7, 8, 13.62
  c 12, 16, 20
  d 6, 7, 9.22
  e 5, 5, 7.07

2 A builder is checking whether he has made a proper right angle on some brickwork. He measures two lengths of 4.5 m and a hypotenuse of 6.36 m. Has he managed a correct right angle?

3 A triangular sail has its hypotenuse of 8 m attached to the mast of a ship. The other two sides of the sail are 3.4 m and 5.2 m long. Is the sail right angled?

4 Is a triangle with sides 8 cm, 15 cm and 17 cm right angled?
Write down other sets of three whole numbers for side lengths that you know will form a right angled triangle.

Section 4: Using Pythagoras' theorem to solve problems
HOMEWORK 35E

1 The shorter sides of a right angled triangle are 5.6 cm and 6.8 cm long.
What is the length of the hypotenuse?

2 Using the dimensions given in the diagram below, find:
  a the length AB
  b the length BC.

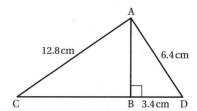

3 Is the triangle in this diagram right angled?
Give a reason for your answer.

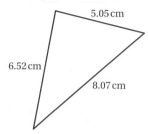

5.05 cm

6.52 cm

8.07 cm

4 The diagram below shows the first three
triangles in 'the wheel of Theodolus', which is
made from a series of right angled triangles.
Find the length of each hypotenuse.

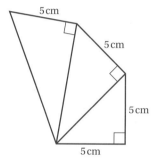

5 cm

5 cm

5 cm

5 cm

5 cm

5 The diagram below shows a trapezium.
Use Pythagoras' theorem to calculate the
dimensions you need to find the area of the
trapezium.

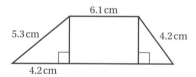

6.1 cm

5.3 cm   4.2 cm

4.2 cm

HOMEWORK 35F

1 On a computer screen a character is 354 pixels
to the right of the bottom left corner and
213 pixels above the bottom edge of the screen.
What is the shortest distance, in pixels, from
the character to the bottom left corner of the
screen?

2 Photographic enlargements are sold in the
following sizes. Work out the length of the
diagonal for each size of photograph.
a 6 inches × 4 inches
b 7 inches × 5 inches
c 8 inches × 10 inches

3 A TV has a screen size of 50 inches across the
diagonal. The screen is 24 inches high, and
has a border around it of 1 inch. What is the
narrowest gap this TV could fit into?

4 The front view of a building is shown in the
diagram below. How tall is the building?

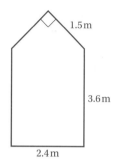

1.5 m

3.6 m

2.4 m

5 A football pitch measures 110 m by 60 m.
What is the diagonal distance across the pitch
from one corner to the other?

6 A surveyor uses a clinometer to measure the
top of a tree to be 25.8 m away from him. The
clinometer is 1.5 m above the ground and the
base of the tree is 15.6 m away.
How tall is the tree?

Chapter 35 review

1 Which of the following triangles are right
angled?
a 5 cm, 6 cm, 8 cm   **b** 9 cm, 12 cm, 15 cm
c 4 cm, 4 cm, 8 cm

2 **a** What is the perimeter of the square below if
the length AB is 4.1 cm?
b What is the area of the square?

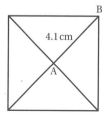

B

4.1 cm

A

3 A ship sails 17.6 km due east then 15.4 km due
south. How far away is the ship from its starting
point?

36 Trigonometry

Section 1: Trigonometry in right-angled triangles

HOMEWORK 36A

1　Find the particular trigonometric ratios for the marked angles in the diagrams below.

　a　Sine ratio

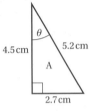

　b　Tangent ratio

　c　Cosine ratio

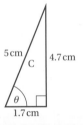

Tip

　Use your calculator for Sections 1, 3 and review.

2　For the angle shown in the triangle below, find:
　a　the sine ratio　　b　the cosine ratio
　c　the tangent ratio.

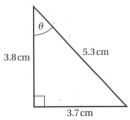

HOMEWORK 36B

1　For each triangle (**a–f**) below, choose the appropriate ratio and find the length of the side indicated. Give your answers to three significant figures.

　a　　　　　　　　　　　　b

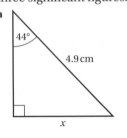
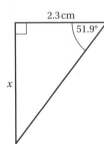

　c

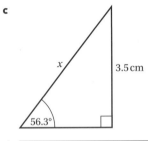

　d

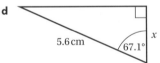

　e　　　　　　　　f

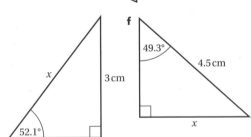

HOMEWORK 36C

1　Calculate the value of each angle given the following ratios.
　a　$\cos \theta = 0.457$　　　b　$\tan \theta = 2.67$
　c　$\sin \theta = 0.867$　　　d　$\tan \theta = 0.896$
　e　$\sin \theta = 0.014$　　　f　$\cos \theta = 0.123$

2 For each triangle (**a**–**f**) below, choose the appropriate ratio and find the size of the angle indicated. Give your answers to one decimal place.

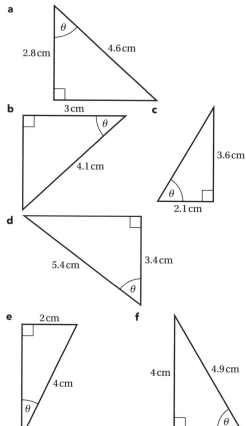

3 The triangle FEA is a right-angled triangle with AE = 2.5 cm and AF = 4.5 cm. Find the size of the angle AFE.

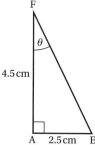

4 **a** What is the size of angle x?

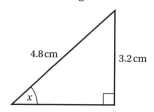

b What would be the size of the angle x if both side lengths were doubled?

5 For each triangle, draw a sketch and then calculate the required values. Give your answers to two decimal places.

a In triangle ABC, the angle A is 90°, the angle C = 40° and the side AB = 7.5 cm. Find the length of BC.

b In triangle PQR, the angle R is 90°, the angle P = 63° and the side PQ = 15.2 cm. Find the length of RQ.

c In triangle ABC, the angle B is 90°, the angle C = 31.4° and the side AB = 17.3 cm. Find the length of BC.

6 For each triangle, draw a sketch and then calculate the required values. Give your answers to two decimal places.

a In triangle XYZ, the angle Y is 90°, YZ = 6.3 cm and XZ = 18.4 cm. Find the angle X.

b In triangle ABC, the angle A is 90°, AB = 8.9 cm and BC = 11.3 cm. Find the angle B.

c In triangle PQR, the angle R is 90°, PR = 17.3 cm and RQ = 18.4 cm. Find the angle P.

Section 2: Exact values of trigonometric ratios
HOMEWORK 36D

1 Write down the exact value of:

a sin 0°   **b** cos 30°   **c** sin 60°
d cos 90°   **e** sin 30°   **f** tan 45°
g cos 0°   **h** tan 60°   **i** sin 45°

> **Tip**
>
> If you don't know these values you should learn them.

2 What is:

a cos 30° + sin 60°?
b cos 60° + sin 30°?
c cos 45° + sin 45°?

101

Section 3: Solving problems using trigonometry
HOMEWORK 36E

1 The diagram below shows a sketch of the cross section of a children's slide. What is the maximum height of the slide?

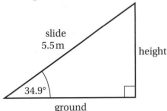

2 A tree surgeon is standing 25 m away from the base of a tree. He measures an angle of 23.1° to the top of the tree from a height of 1.5 m. How tall is the tree?

3 The coastguard is looking down from a cliff 78 m high through a telescope to a boat out at sea. The angle of depression is 26.3° and the telescope is 1.7 m above the cliff top. How far out to sea is the boat?

4 A radio phone mast is 67.3 m tall. It is held in place by wires attached to the top of the mast that make an angle of 78.4° with the ground. How long is each wire?

5 A disabled access ramp is 10 m long and rises 50 cm. What angle does the ramp make with the ground?

6 An aircraft is climbing at a consistent angle of 29.8° to the ground for a distance of 1.8 km through the air. What is the equivalent distance along the ground?

Chapter 36 review

1 The diagram below shows the triangle ABC. Find the size of the marked angle.

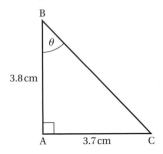

2 The triangle XYZ is shown in the diagram below. Find the length of the other two sides.

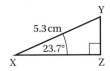

3 A ladder placed 1.75 m away from a wall makes an angle of 73.2° with the ground. How far up the wall does the ladder reach?

4 A fixed crane has a jib of 47.43 m which is leaning at an angle of 36.7° to the ground. How far away from its base can the crane reach?

37 Graphs of other functions and equations

Section 1: Review of linear graphs
HOMEWORK 37A

1 Write the equation of each of the following graphs.
- **a** A line parallel to the y-axis and passing through point (2, 0)
- **b** The set of points with x-coordinate of -3
- **c** The y-axis
- **d** The x-axis
- **e** The line perpendicular to the x-axis at 3
- **f** The line parallel to the x-axis and passing through y at $1\frac{1}{2}$
- **g** The set of all points with y-coordinate of -1

2 Write the equation of each line (**a**–**e**) shown below.

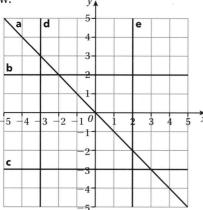

3 Look at the diagram and answer the questions.

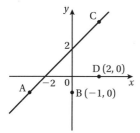

a What is the equation of line AC?

b Given that AB is parallel to the *x*-axis, what is the equation of a line through points A and B?

c Given that CD is parallel to the *x*-axis, what would be the equation of a line joining these points?

Section 2: Quadratic functions
HOMEWORK 37B

1 Copy and complete this table for the given values of *x*.

x	**–3**	**–2**	**–1**	**0**	**1**	**2**	**3**
$y = 2x^2$							
$y = \frac{1}{2}x^2$							
$y = -2x^2$							
$y = -\frac{1}{2}x^2$							

2 Use the completed table of values from question 1 to plot the four graphs on the same system of axes. Use a different colour for each graph.

3 Use your graphs from question 2 to answer these questions.

a What are the coordinates of the point where each graph turns?

b Are the graphs symmetrical about the *y*-axis? Give a reason for your answer.

c Compare the width of the graphs. What do you notice?

d Why are two graphs above the *x*-axis and two graphs below it?

HOMEWORK 37C

1 Identify the features labelled (**a**–**d**) in the graphs shown below.

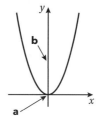
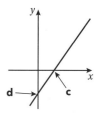

2 For each of the graphs (A–F) below, identify:

a the turning point and whether it is a maximum or minimum

b the axis of symmetry

c the *y*-intercept

d the *x*-intercepts.

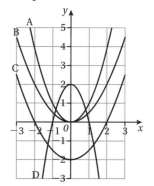

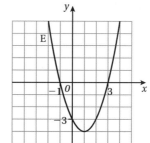
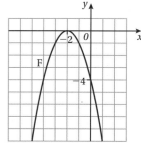

3 Each statement below this graph is **false**.
Identify the mistakes and correct the
statements.

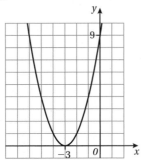

a The axis of symmetry is $y = -3$.
b The turning point is a maximum at $(9, 0)$.
c The x-intercepts are $(0, 9)$ and $(-3,0)$.
d The graph doesn't cut the y-axis.

HOMEWORK 37D

1 Draw and label sketch graphs of the following.

a $y = \dfrac{1}{2}x^2 - \dfrac{1}{2}$ b $y = -2x^2 + 8$

c $y = 2x^2 - 3$ d $y = \dfrac{1}{2}x^2 + 2$

2 Use the information on each quadratic graph
(**a–f**) to work out its equation.

a 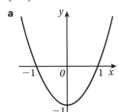   b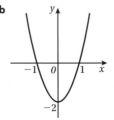

c 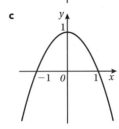   d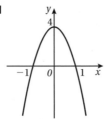

e 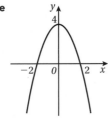   f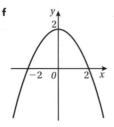

Section 3: Other polynomials and reciprocals

HOMEWORK 37E

1 Draw up a table of values for each equation.
Plot each graph on a separate grid.

a $y = 3x^3$
b $y = 2x^3 - 3$
c $y = 3x^3 + 1$
d $y = \dfrac{1}{2}x^3 + 1$

2 The graph of $y = 2x^3 + 2$ is shown below.
Use this to sketch a graph showing what you
would expect the graph of $y = -2x^3 + 2$ to
look like.

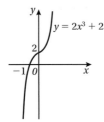

HOMEWORK 37F

1 Draw up a table of values and plot each pair of
graphs on the same system of axes.

a $y = \dfrac{-4}{x}$ and $y = \dfrac{-6}{x}$

b $y = \dfrac{2}{x}$ and $y = \dfrac{6}{x}$

c $xy = 1$ and $xy = 4$

2 Study the two graphs (A and B) of $y = \dfrac{a}{x}$.

A

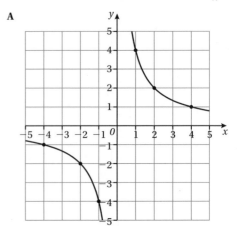

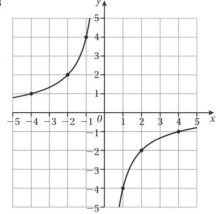

B

a Which graph has a positive value of a? How do you know this?

b Which graph has the line $y = x$ as its line of symmetry?

c What is the equation of each graph?

③ Three reciprocal graphs (A–C) are shown on the grid below. A point is given for each graph.

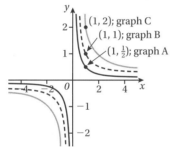

(1, 2); graph C
(1, 1); graph B
(1, $\frac{1}{2}$); graph A

Match each graph to its correct equation.

i $xy = 1$ **ii** $2xy = 1$ **iii** $xy = 2$

④ This is the graph of $y = \frac{4}{x}$, plotted accurately. Use the information in the graph below to plot the graph of $y = \frac{4}{x} + 1$.

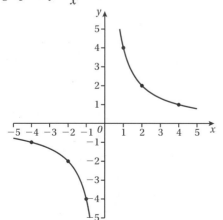

Section 4: Plotting, sketching and recognising graphs

HOMEWORK 37G

① Sketch the following graphs.

a $y = -x + 4$ **b** $x = 9$ **c** $y = x^2$

d $y = -2$ **e** $y = x^3$

② Draw up a table of values and plot each of the following graphs.

a $xy = -15$ **b** $y = \frac{16}{x}$ **c** $y = 2x^3 + 1$

③ Describe each graph (**a–f**) shown below and write the general form of its equation, using the letter k to represent any constant values.

a
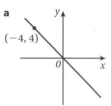
$(-4, 4)$

b
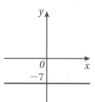
-7

c
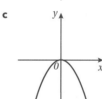

d
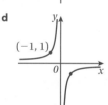
$(-1, 1)$

e
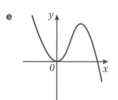

f
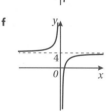
4

Chapter 37 review

① Read each statement. Decide whether it is true or false. If it is false, write a correct version.

a The graph of $xy = k$ is the same as the graph of $y = \frac{k}{x}$

b $2x^2 - 3y + 1 = 0$ is a straight line graph with a gradient of $\frac{2}{3}$

c The graph $x = k$ is a straight line parallel to the x-axis.

d The standard equation $y = ax^3 + bx + c$ will produce a cubic curve.

e $y = 3x^2$ is a U-shaped graph with the y-axis as its axis of symmetry.

2 Sketch each of the following graphs.
   a $y = x$ b $y = 2$ c $y = \dfrac{-1}{x}$
   d y^2 e $y = -x + 2$ f $y = \dfrac{2}{x} + 1$
   g $y = 2x$ h $xy = 2$ i $y = -x^3 + 1$

38 Growth and decay

Section 1: Simple and compound growth

HOMEWORK 38A

1 Calculate the simple interest on:
   a £700 invested for two years at the rate of 15% per annum
   b £800 invested for eight years at the rate of 7% per annum
   c £5000 invested for 15 months at the rate of 5.5% per annum.

> **Tip**
>
> 'Per annum' means 'each year'.
> It is sometimes shortened to 'pa'.

2 £7500 is invested at 3.5% per annum simple interest. How long will it take for the amount to reach £8812.50?

3 The total simple interest on £1600 invested for five years is £224. What is the percentage rate per annum?

4 Calculate the compound interest on:
   a £700 invested for two years at the rate of 15% per annum
   b £800 borrowed for eight years at the rate of 7% per annum
   c £5000 borrowed for 15 months at the rate of 5.5% per annum.

5 How much will you have in the bank after four years if you invest £500 for four years at 3% interest, compounded annually?

6 Mrs Genaro owns a small business. She borrows £18 500 from the bank to finance some new equipment. She repays the loan in full after two years. If the bank charged her compound interest at the rate of 21% per annum, how much did she repay over the two years?

Section 2: Simple and compound decay

HOMEWORK 38B

1 The value of a computer system at the time of installation is £9500. The system decreases in value by £1500 per annum. What is its value after four years?

2 A car costing £10 000 depreciates in value by 10% per year. What is the car worth after seven years?

3 The number of applications at a college is reducing by 8% per annum. If 3800 applications were received in 2014, how many applications would you expect to have in 2018?

4 In 2010 there were an estimated 1600 giant pandas in China. Calculate the likely giant panda population in 2025 if there is:
   a an annual growth in the population of 0.5%
   b an annual decline in the population of 0.5%.

5 The value of a security system at the time of installation is £8400. If the company calculates depreciation on a reducing balance at 15% per annum, what is the system worth four years after it is installed?

Chapter 38 review

1. A woman invests £5000 in an investment scheme for five years and earns 8% pa simple interest.

   a Calculate the total interest she will earn.

   b How much would she need to invest to earn £3600 interest in the same period (at the same rate)?

   c At the end of an investment period, the woman is told her £5000 has increased in value by 23%. Use a multiplier to work out how much the investment is worth at the end of this period.

2. The table below compares the simple and compound interest earned on £10 000 invested at a rate of 9% pa.

   a Complete the last two columns of the table.

   b What is the difference between the simple interest and compound interest earned after five years?

Years	1	2	3	4	5	6	7	8
Simple interest	900	1800	2700	3600	4500	5400		
Compound interest	900	1881	2950.29	4115.82	5386.24	6771.00		

3. An investment of £9500 does very badly and the client loses money at a rate of 20% per annum. What is the investment worth after four years?